Childhood in question

MANCHESTER
UNIVERSITY PRESS

Childhood in question

Children, parents and the state

edited by
Anthony Fletcher and Stephen Hussey

Manchester University Press
Manchester and New York
distributed exclusively in the USA by St. Martin's Press

Published by Manchester University Press
Oxford Road, Manchester M13 9NR, UK
and Room 400, 175 Fifth Avenue, New York, NY 10010, USA
http://www.man.ac.uk/mup

Distributed exclusively in the USA by
St. Martin's Press, Inc., 175 Fifth Avenue, New York,
NY 10010, USA

Distributed exclusively in Canada by
UBC Press, University of British Columbia, 6344 Memorial Road,
Vancouver, BC, Canada V6T 1Z2

British Library Cataloguing-in-Publication Data
A catalogue record for this book is available from the British Library

Library of Congress Cataloging-in-Publication Data applied for

ISBN 0 7190 5393 5 *hardback*
     0 7190 5394 3 *paperback*

First published 1999

06 05 04 03 02 01 00 99   10 9 8 7 6 5 4 3 2 1

Typeset in Sabon
by Action Publishing Technology Limited, Gloucester
Printed in Great Britain
by Bell & Bain Ltd, Glasgow

Contents

List of contributors

Lynn Abrams is a senior lecturer in the Department of History at the University of Glasgow.

Elizabeth Buettner is a lecturer in the Department of History at the University of London, Royal Holloway.

Anna Davin is a research fellow in the School of History at Middlesex University.

Anthony Fletcher is Professor in the Department of History at the University of Essex.

Elizabeth A. Foyster is a lecturer in the Department of History at the University of Dundee.

Julie Gammon is a research student in the Department of History at the University of Essex.

Ralph Houlbrooke is a reader in the Department of History at the University of Reading.

Stephen Hussey is Essex County Council Lecturer in Oral History in the Department of History at the University of Essex.

Louise A. Jackson is a lecturer in history in the School of Cultural Studies at Leeds Metropolitan University.

Heather Shore is the Moses and Mary Finley Research Fellow at Darwin College, Cambridge University.

Acknowledgements

The chapters included in this book all began life as papers presented to the 'Childhood in Question' conference held at the Department of History at the University of Essex, 18–20 April 1997. The editors would like to acknowledge the generous support offered to the conference by the Istituto per gli studi Filosofici, Naples. Within the Department of History our thanks are due to Cathy Crawford, Geoff Crossick, Joan Davies, Julie Gammon, Philip Hills, Anne Kemp-Luck, Lauren Pitcher, Kevin Schürer, Fiona Venn, John Walter and Belinda Waterman. At Manchester University Press Louise Edwards, Carolyn Hand and Gemma Marren lent support, advice and encouragement.

Stephen Hussey would also like to acknowledge the support, help and friendship given to him by Julia Rankin.

1 *Anthony Fletcher and Stephen Hussey*

Introduction

This book is about various aspects of the experience of children in Britain at times between the middle of the seventeenth century and the 1960s. It tackles the least explored aspect of British childhood studies. Indeed one historian has commented that the actual world of early modern childhood is 'now largely impenetrable', except through scant survivals of personal testimony in diaries and autobiographies.[1] The case studies offered here do not rest on this kind of source material; they draw instead on information in legal and welfare records and on publications reporting about children's experience. The exception is the use of correspondence in Elizabeth Buettner's account of the Talbot family. The book raises major issues of historical methodology and about reaching into the minds and emotions of children through the use of second-hand material.

This Introduction aims to sketch the context by reviewing recent work on parenting and on ideas about childhood which, as they have changed and developed, have evidently made some impact on upbringing though it is hard to take the measure of this. Regarding all such matters, debate over the last twenty or so years has been lively and sometimes contentious. A guide to and commentary upon this debate sets the scene for the specific and detailed studies which follow and which, it is hoped, will inspire further work on the most difficult but fascinating question at stake in this field.

Some have argued that the historian should not be attempting to retrieve childhood experience from the past. In this respect,

Carolyn Steedman has written of those that are 'doggedly determined to track down what is in fact lost and gone', and of the futility of 'a search that is hopeless yet compulsive'.[2] It is important to acknowledge that our own remembered childhood and perceptions of what childhood experience does and should incorporate cannot be disentangled from those that we study. Yet much still remains, particularly in relation to the ways in which children have been viewed and conceptualised in the past. Hugh Cunningham has traced the process since 1500, which he calls the development of a middle-class ideology of childhood. He stresses how Protestant advice books for parents emphasised original sin, teaching them to see their children as a source of anxiety as well as joy, since their wills had to be broken and their innate propensity to evil had to be eradicated. It is now well established that it was in the eighteenth century that people began to see childhood as a stage of life to be valued in its own right. John Locke's *Some Thoughts Concerning Education*, published in 1693, originated in a series of letters of advice to a gentleman about bringing up his son. The premise here, more fully explored in *An Essay Concerning Human Understanding*, was that the child's mind is a tabula rasa or blank sheet, whereas in abilities or temperament he was an individual and to be treated as such. This was an important step, and yet, as Cunningham remarks, Locke's incipient child-centredness was tempered by his insistence on parents producing adults who conformed to their class and gender roles. Rousseau, in *Emile* published in 1762, was more radical. Whereas Locke advised parents to develop the child's capacity for reason, Rousseau would have them abandon this objective, for childhood, as he declared, had 'its own ways of seeing, thinking and feeling', which could be allowed full expression by a child's being brought up in the ways of nature. Rousseau, in this sense, helped to give birth to romanticism which, as a body of ideas, transformed thinking about childhood in the early nineteenth century. The classic text was William Wordsworth's *Ode on Intimations of Immortality from Recollections of Early Childhood*. At the heart of the message of the Lake District poet was a reverence for and sanctification of childhood: 'from being the smallest and least considered of human beings', as Cunningham has put it, 'the child had become endowed with qualities which made it Godlike, fit to be worshipped, and the embodiment of hope'. Yet there were many cross-currents, such as the evangelical movement and the public-school tradition: childrearing at the practical level in Victorian Britain was not based upon romanticism as such but was more hard-headed than this. At the same time the legacy of romanticism was profound, informing the campaigns to save the children which underlie the essays by Louise Jackson and Lynn Abrams in this volume.[3]

All this is fairly clear-cut and uncontentious. The case with regard to parenting, the issue that has dominated childhood studies recently, is quite different. In his massive and influential study of *The Family, Sex and Marriage in England 1500–1800*, published in 1977, Lawrence Stone built an argument on the severe Protestant advice literature of the late sixteenth and early seventeenth centuries. He ruthlessly turned prescription into practice, without adducing any appreciable body of primary evidence to support his views. His case was that 'a remarkable change' had occurred in child-rearing theory and standard child-rearing practices between 1660 and 1800, producing more persuasive and child-oriented parent–child relations.[4] Stone's story, and in this he was at one with others like Lloyd de Mause and Edward Shorter, was a story of progress based upon decisive changes in attitudes to and treatment of children.[5] Linda Pollock's *Forgotten Children* published in 1983, was an effective critique of Stone's work, attacking it for being methodologically unsound and mistaken in its conclusions. Basing her account upon a systematic study of diaries and autobiographies from Britain and North America concerning childrearing over four hundred years, Pollock argued for continuity in love and affection rather than a change from harshness to permissiveness.[6] Others such as Ralph Houlbrooke and Keith Wrightson have strongly supported Pollock's stance.[7] Indeed, it can now be stated with some conviction that the majority of parents were concerned about, involved with and affectionate towards their children during the whole of the period that this book covers, even if changing conventions sometimes affected how their love and concern were shown. Parenting, in other words, is something that adults have in general, over the last four hundred years, taken seriously as well as rejoiced in. The historian's itch to see linear change and recognise progress in history has probably in this field been substantially misleading and mystifying.

So this is our easiest point of entry to the child's world, taking it from the other side of the fence so to speak. We can gain insight in specific cases from parental records into the culture and atmosphere of relationships and into behaviour at home, even if this is usually achieved through reported speech. Thus Nehemiah Wallington, the London artisan, keeping his diary for October 1625, recorded in an entirely matter-of-fact way the bedtime chatter of his young daughter Elizabeth: 'at night when we were abed says she to me "Father I go abroad tomorrow and buy you a plum pie"'. What could be more spontaneous and simply affectionate than these words? They are recalled, cherished and recorded because, as it turned out, they were the last words she uttered. The plague was rife in London that autumn; the following morning Elizabeth was in agony, forty-eight hours later she was dead.[8]

What do we make of four-year-old Alice Thornton consoling her mother at her brother's death in 1660? She 'looked very seriously on me', the mother records, and said 'my dear mother, why do you mourn and weep so much for my brother Willy? Do you not think he is gone to heaven?' Alice Thornton, one suspects, tells us about her child, another Alice's words because she wants to keep a clear hold on her own faith, expressed in her reply to the four-year-old, and on the full significance of Willy's death for the family: 'Yes, dear heart, I believe he is gone to heaven, but your father is so afflicted for his loss and, being a son, he takes it more heavily because I have not a son to live.' She then expands on her child's further protestations and pleas for patience in adversity, because the interlocution has proved comforting and supportive to her. But, for this very reason, we cannot place faith in the precocious child having really said exactly what her mother alleges her to have done. What we probably can say is that this child, reared in a strongly puritan home, had an unquestioning childhood faith. Her mother, instructed, as she says, 'by the mouth of one of my own children', attempted to heed little Alice's innocent words.[9] Alice Thornton was fond of using her children as a mouthpiece for the tenets that she herself held dear and wished to inculcate in others. Her son, Robin, she noted in 1668, 'one day, being about four years old, he told me of his own accord that God was a pure, holy, wise and merciful spirit; but the devil was a wicked, lying, malicious spirit'. Even if the speech is not quite accurately reported, such a passage does provide insight into the mental structure that strict Protestantism created in the minds of the very young. Little Robin Thornton learnt to see himself as a being easily at the mercy of the personified occult forces of good and evil. This, rather than a strong sense of his own identity, individuality or potential, was what most power-fully informed his growing up.[10]

Two further examples from the early modern period will reit-erate the point that personal sources of this kind are invaluable for lighting up the realities of childhood experience in the past. Everyone tends to think of childhood, their own and other people's, as a time of freedom, happiness and pleasure. The Presbyterian minister Henry Newcome wrote down his thoughts in middle age, reflecting on boyhood days through the prism of his serious adult faith. It was the weather, a soft rain typical of autumn, that reminded him on 21 October 1666 of Sunday games of bandy-ball, a primitive kind of hockey, seeing this now as a sin of his youth yet recalling all the fun of it at the same time: 'the time, the place, the person, the weather, may make one's heart sad in such remembrances'. In the following September he noted how 'we walked abroad and nutted' and this put him through the same mental process of self-reflection: 'it put me in mind of my youth; and might have minded me of sin, in that sometimes on the Lord's day, when a child, I had done so'.[11]

What is exceptional before 1700 is the survival of an authentic boyhood diary with the immediacy this offers of day-to-day living, such as that of Thomas Isham, oldest son of Sir Justinian Isham. He grew up on his father's estate at Lamport in Northamptonshire. Young Thomas, encouraged by his intellec-tual father's promise of six pounds a year 'if I would describe in writing whatever happened each day', provides a wonderfully detailed account of an intimate country world, but he never says anything directly about his feelings. Yet we can infer from what he recounts in 1671 that he was building his identity as a landowner and a man of standing in his neighbourhood. He patronises unthinkingly, noting one day how 'the country feasts were celebrated according to custom' and another how little the men of nearby Houghton knew in killing a white cock: it 'had one of his spurs violently wrenched off and died, from which it is clear that the men of Houghton are indeed rustic and completely igno-

rant of learning not to remember that trite saying "never lay
hands on a white cock"'. Thomas learnt about managing the
estate, joining his father for example in the fields 'to decide where
new ditches should be dug and hedges set'. His studies were
pursued at home, managed by his father and a resident tutor. He
was alive to the animals – the hound Sissa's eleven puppies – and
to the family. The servant's expedition to Northampton to buy
cloth for his eight-year-old brother's first breeches receives a
mention. It was an active and vigorous life, peopled by friends of
the family and neighbours, duly ranked by social distinctions.
When someone tells you so much about what he did and experienced each day, even though the narrative is entirely unreflective,
the historian has the chance to reconstruct the patterns of a childhood and say something about its mental and emotional realities.
But material of this quality from any time before 1900 is very
rare.[12]

The period covered by the essays in this book saw a huge epis-
temological shift. The mental worlds of the children who inhabit
the accounts of Ralph Houlbrooke on the one hand and Lynn
Abrams on the other are so entirely different that there is a gulf
fixed across the volume. It is a gulf that has been well explored by
historians and philosophers: the gulf between modernity, now
itself under challenge, and pre-modernity. Bacon, Descartes,
Locke and Montaigne are among the key transitional figures. A
fundamental account of the making of modern identity is
provided by Charles Taylor in his book *Sources of the Self*. He
argues that modern subjectivity has its roots in ideas of human
good.[13] Danah Zohar is among those who have written with
particular insight about the impact of Cartesianism, suggesting
that in the modern world we are mostly good Cartesians at heart.
That is we have learnt and been brought up to experience
ourselves as a self which has or is within a body: 'we feel
ourselves', she writes, 'to be deeply private, tucked away, an
intangible something that peeks out at the wider world beyond
and which might enjoy all manner of capacities and freedoms but
for the body's limitations'.[14] Historians have only just begun to
explore how a new sense of self was beginning, in the late seventeenth century, to become a crucial part of what is distinctive,
modern and western about man. Locke's innovation, as Roger
Smith notes, was to detach the question of personal identity from

theology and associate it with consciousness. At much the same time, Descartes was prompting the examination of the individual mind as a source of knowledge and stressing self-examination as an individual, as opposed to a social, performance.[15] Jonathan Sawday has explored interiority and selfhood from the point of view of the period's engagement with embodiment.[16] Peter Burke has written about the concepts of the self that emerged from Renaissance thinking, about biography and autobiography, portrait and self-portrait at this time.[17]

There were all these directions and signposts towards modernity, but the simple fact is that, to understand the significance of the arguments presented by Ralph Houlbrooke (chapter 3) and Elizabeth Foyster (chapter 4), we need to be clear that they are writing about an essentially pre-modern mental world and society. They are both quite explicit about this. Elizabeth Foyster portrays her silent witnesses to the breakdown of domestic and social order as in a kind of quarantine. They were not assumed to have any sort of developed sense of self, to be emotionally involved in traumatic incidents that they watched and absorbed at home, or to be capable of describing or reflecting upon such incidents as witnesses in court. As she explains, this was because children at that time, and before Locke's thinking had made its impact, were not acknowledged as having active and developing emotional lives and were not seen as vulnerable to psychological damage in childhood in the way they are today.

Ralph Houlbrooke presents us with James Janeway, author of *A Token for Children* published in 1671. He argues that he was a man who genuinely believed children were not too young to be damned. He collected information about and narrated the deaths of some thirteen youngsters who showed spiritual precocity. These case studies enabled Janeway to sustain his argument about the authenticity of children's deep religious experience. Janeway, in Houlbrooke's reasoning, was neither a dramatist given to exaggeration nor a fantasist, but a sober nonconformist minister with an evangelical message he wanted to put across. There is no claim that Janeway's subjects are typical. Parents who may have looked for spiritual understanding in their children on their deathbeds and failed to find it are cited. But Houlbrooke's basic point is that the experiences, which Janeway recounts, are authentic. For wherein did the identity of these children consist? Lacking any glimmerings of the modern conception of the self and of personal identity, brought up in severe puritan homes, they were likely to become obsessive about the struggle between good and evil in the kind of way that Janeway describes. They were in a sense puppets on their parental strings. They had absorbed a literal belief in the afterlife that provided emotional sustenance; their anxieties focused upon the fact that there was an alternative more terrifying place to heaven where they might go. Yet, as Houlbrooke convincingly argues, a boy like Richard Evelyn, unafraid to die, reflects the security a youngster could attain through the 'as yet unbroken and unquestioned consistency and coherence of the universal picture that the elder Evelyn presented to his son'. It is in no way surprising that in some cases a sheltered domestic world built on utterly sure faith enabled young children to develop the kind of spiritual precocity that Janeway illustrates. At the same time, there are hints here that, the more precocious the child, the more likely he was to cling to the rituals which seemed to construct and reiterate his parents' faith. This is the significance of the fact that Houlbrooke finds the most precocious of all the thirteen unable to endure being put to bed before family prayers and scripture reading. He is recorded as having reminded his parents of this. Evidence adduced by Houlbrooke about the imaginative reality of heaven for some children, such as Tom Josselin's dream about being drawn up into heaven by Jesus Christ and Mary Martindale's frequent talk of heaven and being buried by her dead brother, supports his argument about the authenticity of the material that James Janeway presents. This chapter shows how much it is possible for us to learn about the real experience of children in the past even though we are dealing here entirely with reported speech.

The children who appear in Elizabeth Foyster's account of marital disorder in the late seventeenth century were not, as we have seen, understood as having emotional lives although no doubt they did so. Two hundred years later all this was different. This is vividly illustrated by the experience of Guendolen Talbot, during her time at English boarding schools when her parents were in India in the 1880s and 1890s. Elizabeth Buettner's chapter shows how the general experience of growing up in middling and upper-class families had been transformed. This transformation can be summarised by saying that Guendolen, at home with her parents until the age of five and then sent to England for schooling, had imbibed the notion that she deserved and her parents owed her a proper childhood. What this meant was family closeness and affection and parents and children spending time and enjoying things together. The argument is not that this closeness and affection was entirely lacking in seventeenth-century families, but that it had become more studied, more self-conscious and perhaps more intense. Consider the ideal which their aunt expressed in a self-congratulatory letter to the girls' father after Guendolen and Muriel Talbot had spent some while at her home before going to boarding school: 'I can conscientiously say that they have been far more anxiously and affectionately watched over than had they been elsewhere.' Much development had taken place in positive thinking about fatherhood and motherhood since the late seventeenth century. Parenting responsibilities were now discussed, pondered and thought about just as childhood, as we have seen, was idealised.[18] Parents were thus motivated to develop a keen intimacy with their offspring and when this was then broken by distance, as it was in the case of Guendolen and Muriel Talbot, the effect was devastating. Guendolen's cry that, as a ten-year-old boarder, there was 'no-one to comfort me here' and nobody she could talk with 'like I would to you' was heartfelt. The striking image she used the following year – 'I feel as if you were kind of locked up toys that one could not have' – shows how hard she found the separation to bear. Guendolen had learnt to expect much; she may have missed her parents with a greater intensity than children had normally done in earlier centuries because of this early experience. Expectations were particularly high regarding holidays, unknown in the seventeenth century. Thus a month at Brighton with three old fogey schoolmistresses, instead of their parents, was almost too much for the four Talbot girls to cope with.

Julie Gammon's material about juvenile victims of rape (chapter 5) reiterates Elizabeth Foyster's point regarding children's emotions: even in the eighteenth century, there was little grasp of childhood sensibility. Thus the child raped was seen in court in the hard and fast terms of an adult before her time, because the rape had deprived her of her innocence. She was treated as if she was capable of showing much more understanding of legal proceedings and of giving more accurate testimony in court than in fact was likely. No clear distinction was made between what might be expected from her as a witness and from the adults around her. At the same time, Gammon does find some evidence of a growing sense of the responsibility parents could be expected to show about guarding their girls against vulnerable situations in which they were alone with men. Yet this sense of responsibility had by no means penetrated society as a whole. Children were raped because they were not adequately protected. The chapter sheds shafts of light upon the experience, though it hardly touches the actual emotions that must have been involved. Eleven-year-old Mary Homewood worked as a pot-girl in the public house owned by her father. She was obviously terrified of what might happen if she refused to deliver beer to the nearby dyehouse, where her assailant David Scott worked. She told the court that she was afraid her parents would beat her. As it was, she took the beer, tried to push Scott off but found him too strong for her, was raped and then was beaten as well when her mother flew into a rage with her rather than listening to her story. We can only imagine the terror she suffered. The servant-girl Mary Matthews went through a similar ordeal, only in her case she believed her master and mistress would dismiss her, holding her responsible for what had happened, and that her parents would beat her as well if she confessed the story.

Men intent on sex with young girls were capable of every kind of manipulation, threat and intimidation. Eleven-year-old Susan Marshall, asked why she did not cry out when Julian Brown sought to rape her in 1735, declared, we are told, that 'he gave me a dram of aniseed and I shall have a pretty baby of my own to nurse and that will be better than crying out'. The words were evidently taken as proof that, in knowing that intercourse might lead to pregnancy, Susan was far from innocent. Much was made of this in discrediting her account. Maria Cummings, 150 years later, showed rather more strength in resisting her father's advances, but was thrown down on the floor and raped almost literally at knife point. The change in public attitudes is signified by the fact that in this case her father was sentenced to twenty years of penal servitude.

Both Julie Gammon and Louise Jackson base their chapters on court records so both therefore face the same issues about authorial voice in the use of depositions. Jackson (chapter 8) makes her position more explicit than Gammon but both share the same common-sense assumptions. She warns about taking care over treating depositions 'simply as a verbatim report of a witness's original story', claiming, nevertheless, that they are a valuable untapped source which 'do tell us a great deal about how people reacted to moments of crisis and made sense of experiences'. Jackson's account of the case of John Thurlow and the sexual relationship with his thirteen-year-old daughter Lily, as it was revealed in Clerkenwell police court in 1885, is both vivid and entirely authentic in this respect. It is the tone, detail and specificity of Lily's version of events that convinces us that we are close to the heart of the actual experience she had undergone: 'I have been afraid to move and speak when he has done it because of his threats'; the incident of the promise of a doll in Seven Sisters Road; his demands at bedtime that night; her revelation of his behaviour in a note to her mother put under her pillow. If Jackson's account illuminates aspects of childhood experience in some particular instances it also touches interestingly upon parental responsibility, the other main theme of this volume. She comments on the key role of parents in discovering and reporting incidents of sexual abuse and the existence of a set of common cultural, social and moral codes, by the late nineteenth century, which enabled them to pursue the perpetrators of abuse. The need some women felt in cases within the family to protect their husbands, of course, cut across this. Yet what is clear is that we are here in a world where saving children from cruelty and abuse was a well-established public preoccupation that most adults had learnt to take seriously.

The children who appeared in court in the accounts of Foyster and Gammon can be seen in some sense as victims of the legal system: that is respect for their individual personalities and their emotional lives was lacking. Heather Shore's investigation of juvenile crime in the early nineteenth century (chapter 6) indicates the broad changes in public attitudes to children that were by then taking place. Those in authority saw the emerging problem of juvenile delinquency in stark class terms, focusing their attention on poverty, inadequate parenting and the peer pressure of the street. Yet, at the same time, there were glimmerings of interest in what it had been that had drawn particular working-class children into petty crime. The very fact that she is able to exemplify the vulnerability of teenage boys with her stories of the vigorous but frustrated manhood of those like Thomas Keefe and Philip Hall is in itself significant. The 1816 *Report* on juvenile delinquency in London was a serious attempt to amass information and detect causation on the basis of numerous case histories. These are real children caught up in dysfunctional families, caught up in the kind of desperate parenting which resorted to depriving teenagers of their clothes so they would not go out. The chapter provides considerable insight into the motives of these children and the appeal of street life.

Lynn Abrams treats the central theme of the book, children's subjectivity, through an examination of the trauma of being cared for in foster homes or orphanages in twentieth-century Scotland (chapter 9). The idea of saving children, or protecting and securing their right to protection and care, she shows, had an emotional as well as a physical content to it in Scotland as early as 1864, when the Glasgow City Children's Committee reflected upon the 'buoyancy of spirit' and 'happiness of countenance' to be found in boarded-out children. Yet the reality, as she goes on to show, was not necessarily a sharp contrast between the experience of being fostered and that of the institutionalised orphanage. What is so interesting about the authentic personal material in her chapter, when grown adults look back on the experience of growing up elsewhere than in their natural family, is the modern awareness of a right to a childhood as a time of personal development. In the foster home or orphanage children usually had to submerge their personality, cope as best they could by keeping to the rules, not expect the kind of love and affection which would lift them up in confidence and the joy of living. The experience inculcated wariness and defensiveness: 'you lost a lot in your life afterwards', as one plaintive comment puts it. In a century which Hugh Cunningham has called the 'century of the child', those who lost their childhood have suffered doubly. Lynn Abrams' account brings home the full meaning of this. She makes us aware of the huge impact, now easily taken for granted, of child psychopathology upon the thinking about and treatment of children. In this respect more has changed in the last fifty years than in the previous three hundred.

The book is intended to promote and stimulate further research. It does not pretend to do more than cast some shafts of light into a field of history that is only beginning to be charted. The framework, as Anna Davin suggests (chapter 2), must surely be a constant reiteration of the difficult question 'what is a child?' In attempting to assess children's own understandings of their childhood in the past, the historian faces great obstacles and severe difficulties. But the importance of the subject for the social historians and the fascination of the topic surely make the attempt worthwhile.

Notes

1 R. Houlbrooke (ed.), *English Family Life 1576–1716* (Oxford, Oxford University Press, 1988), p. 133.

2 C. Steedman, *Strange Dislocations: Childhood and the Idea of Human Interiority 1780–1930* (London, Virago, 1995), pp. 2, 3.

3 H. Cunningham, *Children and Childhood in Western Society since 1500* (London, Longman, 1995), pp. 41–78.

4 L. Stone, *The Family, Sex and Marriage in England 1500–1800* (London, Weidenfeld & Nicolson, 1977), pp. 150–217, 405–48

5 L. de Mause (ed.), *The History of Childhood* (New York, Psychohistory Press, 1974); E. Shorter, *The Making of the Modern Family* (London, Collins, 1976).

6 L. Pollock, *Forgotten Children: Parent–Child Relations from 1500 to 1900* (Cambridge, Cambridge University Press, 1983), pp. 1–67.

7 R. Houlbrooke, *The English Family 1450–1700* (London, Longman, 1984), p. 156; K. Wrightson, *English Society 1580–1680*, (London, Hutchinson, 1982), p. 118.

8 Houlbrooke, *English Family Life*, pp. 141–2.

9 *Ibid.*, p. 153.

10 *Ibid.*, p. 156.

11 *Ibid.*, pp. 153–4, 156.

12 *Ibid.*, pp. 163–6.

13 C. Taylor, *Sources of the Self: The Making of Modern Identity* (Cambridge, Mass., Harvard University Press, 1989), especially chapters 8–12.

14 D. Zohar, *The Quantum Self* (London, Flamingo, 1991), pp. 74–5.

15 R. Smith, 'Self-reflection and the Self', in R. Porter (ed.), *Rewriting the Self: Histories from the Renaissance to the Present* (London, Routledge, 1997), pp. 49–60.

16 J. Sawday , 'Self and Selfhood in the Seventeenth Century', in Porter

(ed.), *Rewriting the Self*, pp. 29–48; see also J. Sawday, *The Body Emblazoned: Dissection and the Human Body in Renaissance Culture* (London, Routledge, 1995).

17   P. Burke, 'Representations of the Self from Petrarch to Descartes', in Porter (ed.), *Rewriting the Self*, pp. 17–28.

18   See, e.g., L. Davidoff and C. Hall, *Family Fortunes* (London, Hutchinson, 1987), pp. 321–56; J. Tosh, 'Authority and Nurture in Middle-Class Fatherhood: The Case of Early and Mid-Victorian England', *Gender and History*, 8 (1996), 48–64.

What is a child?

The problem with childhood as an analytical term is that it is too familiar. We have all been children; we all know children; some of us have had children, brought them up or taught them. We all 'know' what we mean by child and childhood.

Yet its properties are multiple and elusive; its limits elastic, There is no absolute definition of childhood, whether subjective or official, because it is always lived and defined in cultural and economic contexts. So its character and ideology cannot be taken for granted as 'naturally' or 'normally' this or that: when set beside the experiences of specific children in specific contexts they are full of ambiguity and contradiction. Still more difficult to assess are children's own understandings of childhood, even today, let alone in the past.

But for exactly the same reasons, the effort of research and analysis is worthwhile. Beyond our knowledge that children differ from adults, we recognise that how much they differ, and how, vary with time and place. This quality of contingency can both help us to tease out the history of children and also provide insights into particular historical contexts. Equally, we can learn from the differences in how children and adults see things (about childhood and about life more generally), from the tensions and conflicts between them, and from the variations in how and when children are transformed into adults.

In this chapter I focus on England, on children's place in the last two centuries here, and on what that can tell us about the meanings of childhood. Between the eighteenth and the twentieth centuries an ideal of prolonged and sheltered childhood came to be accepted more and more widely, in the course of other long-term economic, political, social and cultural transformations Changes in the nature and organisation of work concentrated more people into towns, produced a growing separation between paid and unpaid labour, and intensified social differentiation, whether by class, employment and social group, by gender or by age. (Comparable transformations today bring millions of children into the work force of the industrialising countries of the South.)[1]

Eighteenth-century children were generally expected to be useful from an early age, most often in the context of the household as unpaid members of a domestic workforce helping with daily indoor and outdoor chores, agricultural or craft work, and perhaps some form of domestic outwork.[2] As is well known, poor children were extensively employed in the new textile mills in the first decades of industrialisation. In the course of the nineteenth century employers' mutating requirements for profitable output reduced the usefulness of child labour in large-scale production; state intervention placed increasing restraints on its use; and rising real wages meant that the domestic economy had less need of children's earnings.

A popular cult of childhood emerged quite early in the century and thrived on commercial images of rosy-cheeked children at play or of wan, pathetic 'orphans of the storm'. (Peter Coveney drew attention to these developments nearly forty years ago, and Hugh Cunningham and Carolyn Steedman have since explored some of their complexities.)[3]

Towards the end of the nineteenth century greater public value came to be set on human life and health (at least if it was white and of the right 'racial' stock), and thus fuelled state concern with the conditions of childhood, since children's welfare was now seen as relevant to the country's productive and military potential. Meanwhile proliferating experts in medicine, social work and education (new professionals as well as voluntary workers) observed and studied children, and pontificated about 'proper' childhood.[4]

The introduction of compulsory school from the 1870s consolidated the distinctiveness of childhood. From the age of 5 until a leaving age of at least 10, and in most cities up to 14, children by the end of the century had to attend school twice a day five days a week and for most of the year. (In poor urban neighbourhoods, where with younger children school provided a welcome answer to childcare problems, they might start at 3.) This soon eliminated full-time employment for children except perhaps a few in their last school year.

The 1870 Act and subsequent ones consolidating and extending its powers were fuelled partly by the urge to civilise the little heathens of poor neighbourhoods, partly by serious belief in the national and individual benefits of schooling, partly by visions of childhood as a period of carefree dependence or at least of education rather than employment.[5] For poor families, however, compulsory school often made the struggle for daily living still more difficult, since it limited children's ability to help. By the 1890s, as parental confidence grew in the instrumental benefits and even the general usefulness of schooling and as more people's living standards rose, conflict over the priorities for school-age children was diminishing, or survived mainly in more diffuse forms, as with the absence of girls when 'needed at home'. (The school authorities did not generally see children's participation in unpaid, domestic labour as a problem.)[6]

In this general historical framework of the decline of paid child employment and the rise of school, certain themes emerge as significant for the defining of childhood: differences between classes and between ideal and reality; dependence and autonomy; work (paid and unpaid); and state concern with children and the conditions of childhood. I shall start, however, by considering the upper limits of childhood in relation to physiology.

Little people

The most obvious way of identifying a child is physical: the young are for a number of years smaller than adults and without secondary sexual characteristics. But appearances can be deceptive. Individuals do not always 'look their age'. Although physically mature they may never reach intellectual and emotional maturity. Or they can be adult yet look like children, whether because their physical maturing is slow or because it has been halted by genetic or medical conditions. (One student friend of my father's, though in his twenties, had stopped growing at puberty:

publicans always had to be warned in advance when they went for a drink.) Puberty and physical maturity do not happen at a fixed age. And in the assessment of age at a glance, as when tobacconists today decide whether a would-be customer is 'old enough' to be served, there is often room for doubt despite physical and cultural markers of age.

Nor do physical measures of maturity necessarily match up with prevailing (adult) cultural assumptions or with the legal benchmarks for protections or rights. For example, sexual activity often begins well before the age at which sexual activity (or marriage) is permitted in law, let alone by parents. The current age from which sexual intercourse is lawful in Britain is sixteen, but 8,800 'underage' girls became pregnant in 1996.[7]

Again, between societies or social categories the pace of physical development differs. While biological benchmarks of puberty and mature growth are always present, we know from studies both of the past and today that the age at which they are reached varies considerably over time and between groups, and that the factors involved are complex. The age of menarche declined from 20 to 11 over four generations of my own family, across more than a century and spanning Galway, New Zealand, Oxford and London. It seems likely that nutrition standards and social expectations are normally the most important factors, but hormones in the food chain in 1970s Puerto Rico were inducing puberty for some as young as six.

Such potential for variation makes it difficult to say even that childhood ends with puberty. Where children are numerous, families impoverished and underfed, and employment available for the young, some level of quasi-adult independence may precede puberty. Conversely in Britain and other developed countries today dependence on parents is likely to continue well after puberty – into the teens or even the twenties.

Childhood is a period of social and emotional, as well as physical, development. But its upper limits are no easier to establish on psychological grounds. Definitions of mature attitudes and behaviour are social and therefore vary; grown-up individuals can be labelled immature; and indeed psychoanalysis (and today's vogue for listening to the 'inner child') suggests that childhood is never completely left behind.

Big people

If any general definition of childhood is feasible it must be made in relation to adulthood. Children are always, in any culture or society those, who are not yet recognised as adult. Grown-ups approach or reach adult status by leaving childhood; and frequently their adult authority is confirmed through their control or support of children (or both). They remind themselves of their adulthood by reviewing the past they have grown out of. Moreover, the fact that children are relatively helpless, especially in their early years, usually means that they are both dependent on and subordinate to their elders. Their survival depends entirely or partly on adults; adults in return exact obedience and determine how children spend their time, though mutual bonds of love and loyalty usually develop to underpin the relationship, at least in domestic contexts.

Adults at most times therefore have had the power, both generally in society and specifically at home, at work and at school (where that existed), to set the terms of childhood according to their priorities in the present and for the future. Whatever resistance (open or covert) young individuals might attempt, adults are always in a better position to impose their ideas and definitions, their authority in the family buttressed by emotional bonds, in other contexts by their class or function.

Here is a (somewhat extended) example of this. *My Station and Its Duties: A Narrative for Girls going to Service*, by the author of 'The Last Day of the Week', was published in London in 1839. The title page bears the epigraph, 'To do my duty in that station of life unto which it shall please God to call me'. The book describes instruction in the Church of England catechism in a village school, presumably as model more than simple depiction. The first chapter recounts a lesson in which the lady teacher, clearly of superior class, asks the children to consider their station in life, 'in order that they might the better ascertain the duties which they were called upon to fulfil'.

> 'Now tell me, one by one, what is your station of life?'
> There was a long pause, each being anxious to penetrate into the full meaning of the question; but their reply was waited for without further explanation. The first at length said,
> 'My father is a labourer.'

Thus prompted, they all proceeded to declare the different employments in which their fathers were occupied.

'You do not perceive, children,' the lady said, 'that you have not answered my question, which was not, what your *parents*' station is, but what your *own* station is. What is your station, Mary?'

'I haven't got a station.'

'No. Do you not tell me in your Catechism, that a part of your duty to your neighbour is, to do your duty in that state of life unto which it shall please God to call you?'

'Yes, but I'm not called to a station yet.'

'Why do you think so?'

'Because I'm but a child at home.'

'True, but then *that* is your station at present. What is your station?'

'A child at home.'

'What family have your parents at home?'

'I have one brother and two sisters.'

'Then you are a *sister* as well as a *child*.'

'Yes.'

'Where are you now?'

'At school.'

'Then you are a scholar?'

'Yes.'

'Are there any with you at school?'

'Yes, my schoolfellows.'

'Then you are a scholar at school, and a schoolfellow?'

'Do each of you now understand that your stations are those of a child at home, and a sister, and a scholar at school, and a schoolfellow?'

'Yes'; they all answered.

The teacher then goes on to the duties of their station: as children they were to love, honour and obey their parents; as scholars to be obedient, attentive, diligent and regular at school; as sisters and schoolfellows to be loving, meek and kind. They had also to partake of the station of their parents by being honest and industrious.

This does not tell us what the children thought, of course, nor what for them were the parameters of childhood. But it shows the attempt by an adult (of another class) to locate children in a hierarchy of authority, with obligations within and between the strata; and also the recognition that multiple identities and relationships were implied by being a child. The text suggests (without disapproval) that these girls will soon be going into domestic service and although no age is specified for this we can suppose it to be somewhere between 10 and 13. The lady teacher would then give them 'references' no doubt indicating that they had absorbed their lessons in diligence and obedience and were ready to move from the subordination of childhood to that of domestic service (and later of wifehood).[8] Girls of the teacher's own class, on the other hand, would remain daughters and sisters 'at home' unless and until they married, and for a short time only, if at all, be scholars or schoolfellows.

This text belongs to a genre, which continued for several decades to dominate in school readers and some didactic fiction, in which rural hierarchy and peace are idealised and where, young or old, all know their place and their future. Early responsibility is recommended, along with obedience in everything to any elders and betters. It echoes the sentiments and style of the didactic dialogues produced by the evangelical propagandist writer Hannah More from the 1790s.

Despite the echo, by 1839 one would not find in such a text a child like Hannah More's fictional Kate Stanley (in *Coelebs in Search of a Wife*, 1809), a model for (middle-class) readers who proudly abandons childish things at eight: 'I am eight years old today. I gave up all my gilt books, with pictures, this day twelve-month, and today I give up my little story books, and I am now going to read such books as men and women read.'[9] Such precocity was less prized by the middle decades of the nineteenth century, because of the growing trend to expect and cherish childish innocence. Precocity became 'sharpness' (not soft or smooth), unnatural; it even implied danger and corruption. Thus Thackeray's carefully named Becky Sharp (*Vanity Fair*, 1847) was a threat to the innocents of Miss Pinkerton's Academy for Young Ladies. She came from another world, of Bohemian makeshift and disregarded propriety. She was used to adult male company and talk; she knew all about hunger, uncertainty and debt; she was too 'knowing' for a child. Thackeray dryly asks, 'Oh, why did Miss Pinkerton let such a dangerous bird into her cage?' True, being 'an articled pupil' who worked for her education distinguished her from the young ladies who were 'parlour boarders'; even the amiable 'Miss Swartz, the rich woolly-haired mulatto from St Kitts' fitted in better.[10] But still more than lack of funds, her inappropriate upbringing and knowledge, crucial to her character and so to the plot, are what mark her off.

As innocence, ignorance and dependence became increasingly central to definitions of childhood in the domestic vision of the expanding nineteenth-century middle class,[11] however, poor children by the same token were perceived as increasingly less 'childlike'. Children in poor homes of both city and countryside lived hugger-mugger with their elders and with this close view of adult life knew 'too much' about it. They were likely to have some degree of sexual knowledge, and were intimately acquainted with budgeting, hunger, sickness and death. Such children expected to share in the daily work of the home; if domestic survival was a struggle they wanted to play their part. Parents too expected them to do all they could and sometimes more.

Work: as soon as they were able

The capacity to work is not a sufficient measure of difference between child and adult. Where adult life is hard, hands are few and labour is intensive, children are soon called upon. In the world of wages, low status and lack of power expose the unprotected young to particularly intense exploitation, as child and juvenile labour. Overwork in bad conditions means some never reach adulthood; coercion may keep even young adults subservient. Such patterns were obvious during early industrialisation in Britain, the United States and Japan, and there are new variants in parts of the third world today. They tend to confirm the idea that employment in childhood is undesirable.

Exemption from work is likely to be a distinguishing characteristic of childhood where adult labour is plentiful and not under great pressure, especially if children are relatively few in the demographic equation. The more resources available for childcare and the less need for youthful labour, the more childhood may be prolonged and sheltered, and this comes to be seen as defining it. Thus in nineteenth-century Britain economic and cultural factors reinforced each other to enlarge the class gulf between attitudes to childhood.

Middle-class visions notwithstanding, the children of the labouring poor, whether in town or country, continued to live very differently.[12] The cottage children in the lesson above, for example, would undoubtedly help with housework, errands and childcare, gardening, foraging for fuel and wild foods; and quite possibly some agricultural work – weeding and gleaning, scaring birds from crops, feeding any poultry or livestock. In towns children combined unpaid household work with casual paid work in the neighbourhood or (until compulsory school was established) full-time employment in mills, workshops, domestic outwork, domestic service and whatever else might offer.

Sometimes a child might already be useful at an age which to us seems inconceivably young. George Crompton, a child in 1760's Lancashire, later recorded being set to work soon after he learnt to walk, in the domestic manufacture of cotton.

> My mother used to bat the cotton wool on a wire riddle. It was then put into a deep brown mug with a strong ley of soap suds. My mother then tucked up my petticoats about my waist, and put me into the tub to tread upon the cotton at the bottom. When a second riddleful was batted I was lifted out and it was placed in the mug, and I again trod it down. This process was continued until the mug became so full that I could no longer safely stand in it, when a chair was placed beside it and I held on by the back. When the mug was quite full, the soap suds were poured off, and each separate dollop of wool well squeezed to free it from moisture. They were then placed on the bread rack under the beams of the kitchen-loft to dry. My mother and grandmother carded the cotton wool by hand ... When carded they were put aside in separate parcels ready for spinning.[13]

Physical growth only partly determined what a child was permitted or expected to do. Adaptations could be made, like the 'pair of high pattens' which were tied to the feet of a seven-year-old silk-mill worker (William Hutton, born in Derby in 1723) to enable him to reach 'the engine';[14] or the 'light flail' made by his father for ten-year-old John Clare (born in Northamptonshire in 1793) so that they could work together at threshing;[15] or the boxes and chairs on which countless little girls would stand at sinks and tubs. The tasks expected of children might also, then as in some places today, be beyond their strength, resulting at times in exhaustion. stunted growth or injury, at times in long-term deformity, not only in industry but also from heavy domestic labour such as carrying water or fuel or younger siblings.[16]

City children in the nineteenth century worked in a range of contexts. Before compulsory school they might earn their own keep quite young, like the watercress seller interviewed by Henry Mayhew in about 1850, through her mixed contribution of cash, labour and the food provided by employers. ('I ain't a child', she told him, 'and I shan't be a woman till I'm twenty, but I'm past eight, I am.')[17] Mrs Layton, born in Bethnal Green in 1855, was self-sufficient at the age of ten, only sleeping at home: she minded a local shopkeeper's baby and helped in the shop. (When her employer tried to insist she give up her two evening classes at the Ragged School, 'the conflict ended by my refusing to work for her' – she does not mention consulting anyone.)[18] Others assisted or took over from ill, absent, inadequate or deceased parents.[19] Some, casualties where parents had died or fugitives from brutal or exploitative parents, lived a rough and precarious life fending entirely for themselves.

The mid-nineteenth-century working child, then, might have the freedom of the street arab or the burdens of the 'little mother'; might furnish indispensable labour or earnings to a family economy; or, wholly dependent, might 'help' with chores and errands, possibly receiving pocket money. By the early twentieth century that range had narrowed: street arabs had been rounded up and the child's contribution was increasingly seen as 'help' rather than work.

The watercress girl would probably have been gratified by Mayhew's view that 'although only eight years of age [she] had entirely lost all childish ways, and was, indeed, in thoughts and manner, a woman'.[20] But to George Acorn, born about 1885 and writing in 1911, it would have made sense. He believed that poverty and its stresses deprived him of childhood as it 'should' be: 'The worst of the financial stress was that our tender years could not ignore such things. Instead of possessing the light heart of boyhood, I was prematurely old and careworn. I am considerably younger now than I was then.'[21] That poor children were deprived of a proper childhood, careworn and old before their time, was an increasingly frequent comment in reform circles towards the end of the century. It was mobilised in support of kindergarten and child study, of philanthropic projects like the Happy Evening clubs and the Guild of Play; and used, especially by the child-centred socialist Margaret McMillan, to argue for what Seth Koven has called 'civic maternalism' and more state support for children.[22]

Adult children

Early engagement with work does not necessarily mean children 'grow up' faster. If children's labour is a significant resource, adults retain control of it as long as they can, and childhood's deference to authority can be hard to throw off.

Where young people's labour was part of a shared domestic economy to which they were bound by loyalty, duty or perhaps a stake in the future, they might be stuck for years in the contributory and subordinate position of a child though physically and subjectively adult. As apprentices, too, the familial context reinforced their age subordination.

Adult status in early modern times was delayed not only for the apprentice but also for the journeyman. In sixteenth-century Augsburg, Lyndal Roper shows, men attained full adult status only with citizenship, which in turn could require both craft recognition and familial achievement as fathers, as well as mature years and the ownership of property.[23]

Such attitudes prevailed too in the 1930s Clare village described by Conrad Arensberg in *The Irish Countryman* (1937), where the group of 'old men' who exercised informal authority were all 'farm-owners with completed families'; younger men, even in their twenties and thirties, were 'boys'.[24]

For domestic servants up to and beyond the nineteenth century, employment often meant subordination in a familial hierarchy where their social autonomy as adults, especially if female, was denied or attenuated. Nineteenth-century employers claimed the right to supervise and intervene in every detail of their lives – what they wore and how they did their hair, what they read, when and for how long they could leave the house, whom they then saw (and whether visits were allowed) and even what church or chapel they attended. Political maturity was also denied even to male domestic servants by the legal requirement that voters be householders.[25]

Despite the denial of adult prerogatives to servants, however, young servants were not recognised as children. Even during much of the nineteenth century a double standard operated in well-to-do homes. The twelve-year-old nursery maid, for instance, might well be looking after children her own age or older. The teenage skivvy could be on call for longer hours than her employers' children were awake, and expected to perform tasks inconceivable for them, 'far too heavy' even if they were the same age, better fed and more sturdily built. 'Scullery maids are not little girls', Miss Minchin insisted in Frances Hodgson Burnett's *A Little Princess* (1902),[26] though the narrative and author's asides challenge this position. Relationships of class and work were more central to the status of domestic servants than age: as child workers they were deprived of childish privilege, as adults, they lacked adult autonomy. (Echoes of this survived in the colonial context with the use of 'boy' for servant.)

Amongst the better-off, expectation of inheritance, whether of land or other property such as a business, or of an occupational role or a post, might also hold the young adult back from full independence. (In *The Way of All Flesh* [1903] Samuel Butler described how the children of a bullying middle-class patriarch, because of their expensive education, were 'at the mercy of their father for years after they had come to an age where they should be independent', and how he enjoyed 'the fun of shaking his will at them'.)[27] Girls in well-to-do families were in permanent tutelage. They would leave the paternal roof only for marriage, and even the transition from daughter to wife did not necessarily result in adult status: though motherhood might do it. Legally, too, it was often harder for women to achieve full recognition as adults than for men. Take, for instance, in England, the denial of legal status to the married woman or 'feme covert', but also the tendency of nineteenth-century reformers and administrators to lump women and children together.

'Don't treat me like a child'

In the household entirely dependent on its members' earnings, like most in cities from the late nineteenth century on, the balance of power was different. There was a significant watershed when a son or daughter, whatever their previous contribution in work or wage, handed over their first full wage packet. Will Crooks, born in Poplar in 1852, recalled how he watched his mother work late into the night sewing oilskin coats by candlelight, and longed to be a man. He knew himself one at thirteen when work in a black-smith's shop enabled him to give her 5 shillings a week.[28]

For Jane Walsh, born in a Lancashire cotton town in 1905, going full-time was also a big moment. She had first tried for a mill job when she was twelve, but 'was so small and peaky-looking that nobody would take me'. At thirteen she found one 'and was able to leave school'. 'So I came out into the world "educated", grown-up, a wage-earner.

> I remember very well how I celebrated this fact. For years I had been the member of the family dispatched to the pub and the pawnshop, and I had always hated both jobs heartily. I didn't mind going with ordinary messages, or helping with the children; but I loathed going along with the miserable family bundle, to be sneered at and haggled with by the pawnbroker; and beer had done too much damage in our household for me to like the notion of fetching it home.
>
> 'From now on, Mam', I said, clutching my first week's pay, 'you can send our Bernard to the pub and the pawnshop, because I'm not going any more, say what you like.'[29]

Full-time employment gave the new wage-earner more respect and say in the family because it brought ever closer the possibility of departure. It did not always mean greater freedom, especially for girls who were often expected even after a day's work to buckle down to domestic tasks in the evening, ironing or mending for instance. Curfews, too (nine or ten o'clock most often), were commonly in force for young women while they still lived at home, though the bolder would circumvent them.[30] Such constraints contributed to the very high average age of marriage: twenty-six in the early twentieth century.[31]

Official understandings

As now, 'child' in the nineteenth century was a relative term used in two main ways. It specified both 'child-of-parent' and 'child-not-yet-adult'. In the general understanding, children formed a rather wide age cohort linked to biological development: roughly

under 15 or before puberty.[32] But this upper limit of childhood
varied with context, as we have seen, and was being pushed up in
the second half of the century. Protective labour legislation grad-
ually raised the permitted age for first employment (in 1874 it
was made 10 in textile factories, and this was extended in 1878
to workshops and non-textile factories; in 1891 it went up to 11;
in 1901 to 12); and regulated employment of young persons
between 13 and 18. Criminal responsibility could be attributed
from as young as 7; in practice, however, sanctions were increasingly differentiated for those under 16.[33] For legal rights to
inherit, take legal action or vote, infancy ceased only at 21. The
Poor Law counted those over 15 as adult. A mid-century Catholic
mission to East End children used an elastic definition: it was not
'only for children who were going to school, or those under fourteen ... but also, and indeed principally, for big boys and girls
who were at work, up to the age of seventeen and eighteen'.[34] The
1876 Elementary Education Act defined a child as between 5 and
14 years of age, but even in 1900 some rural school boards
allowed children to leave at 10. In the 1908 Children Act 'child'
meant under 14, 'young person' 14 to 16; the Act's provisions
used sometimes 14 and sometimes 16 as upper limits.

Sex made a difference: girls were held to need protection for
longer. For the Prevention of Cruelty Act (1889) and the London
County Council's Public Control Committee in 1900, a child was
a boy under 14 or a girl under 16. The National Society for the
Prevention of Cruelty to Children wanted 16 to be the limit for
both sexes, but 'the common view' according to a London magistrate was 'that a male of fourteen was very nearly independent of
his parents and thus presumably capable of looking out for his
own welfare', and this carried the day.[35] The age of consent
(which affected girls only) was raised from 12 to 13 in 1875,
then to sixteen in 1885, though some social-purity campaigners
argued that 18 or even 21 should be the 'age of female responsibility'.[36]

Over these decades the definition of childhood centred increasingly on the question of dependence. The relation of child to adult
always involved subordination and dependence; but to varying
degrees and with varying age boundaries. In the second half of the
nineteenth century, with dependent and sheltered childhood
firmly established for the middle class, reformers began to extend

similar standards to working-class children, whose lives were seen as in breach of 'proper' childhood. Autonomy, both economic and social, was an adult prerogative. Paid work by children was assumed to mean exploitation by their parents. Children's right was to a 'natural' childhood state of innocence and irresponsibility, and any whose knowledge and responsibility were 'adult' needed rescue.

Orphanage work, 'ragged schools',[37] campaigns against child labour and neglect, penal reform and (especially) expansion of education, all contributed to the process of reducing childhood autonomy and eliminating the independent child. Street arab and substitute mother were rescued; full-time employment was permitted only after the school years; national and local laws restricted other forms of child employment. At the same time, the working-class family economy was being transformed by rising living standards and ideological shifts; children's earnings were becoming less important, and they could be dependent for longer, though their unpaid work remained important in the domestic economy.

Twentieth-century developments

Demographic changes in the twentieth century lowered the ratio of children to adults. This, with the safety net of state benefits developed after the Second World War, further reduced the need for early wage-earning, and in turn reinforced feeling against it. Organised labour also tried to limit the use of youthful workers, in order to protect wage standards based on skill and experience. In recent years youthful dependence has been further lengthened by contracting labour needs in production, high levels of unemployment among school leavers and increased emphasis on training. On the other hand, the demand for low-paid shift employment in the service sector combines sometimes with family need and sometimes with the pressures of consumer culture to push teenagers into Saturday and other part-time work if they can find it.

So the relationship between children and work has changed substantially in all aspects connected with employment – the age at which paid work may begin, the character of that work, its hours and conditions, who makes the decision about starting it, what wages are paid, and who spends them on what.

As regards unpaid work, there has also been much change. The needs which once required hours of work from household members are now met through purchase of goods or of services. Water is on tap; light and heat require no effort and create no mess. The range of domestic livestock needing care has shrunk down to cat or dog, pet rodent, bird or the occasional rabbit. Eggs are not collected; fruit and greens come from market or shop not garden plot. Bought tins, jars, packets and frozen food have replaced the stocks which rural women, helped by children, once preserved, pickled, salted or smoked against the winter. Socks and stockings are bought and seldom even darned. Sewing is taught as a hobby rather than an essential skill; and clothes and household linen are largely bought. Whereas town children used constantly to run round to the corner shop for pennyworths of this and that (or for tobacco or beer), today better storage provision and changed retail practices mean that shopping is more likely done in bulk, by at least one adult, possibly with a car. Provisioning the household is too big a task to be done by children, though they may run the odd errand still.

Responsibility for care of the elderly and invalid no longer rests mainly with family and neighbours; and visits from children to bring them comforts or run their errands or do their chores are less likely than visits from district nurse, home help and social worker, or indeed no visits. Nor is childcare any longer the province of older children: they are supposed to be in school and families are generally smaller. Still more important the pressures of child-rearing theory and of professional advice or even supervision have increased the load of responsibility and designated it as a wholly adult charge. The eight-year-old full-time little mother has given way to the teenager who sometimes baby-sits of an evening (for the eight-year-old perhaps).

Across British cultures, it is widely held that children 'naturally' prefer fun over responsibility and that this should be indulged if possible. Such phrases as 'you're only young once' imply that work and responsibility are wholly undesirable and that it is to be expected and understood that children will not want to help. Their dependence on adults is thus intensified. It is also heightened by the ever-growing range of expensive consumer items promoted and accepted as indispensable for the young (including teenagers). And the emphasis for parents is on buying children 'the best', or indulging their desire for the latest design or fad being promoted. So the old economy of making and repairing and of hand-me-downs is in disfavour, while the costs of parenting increase. Yet these changes are more complete for some than for others. Second-hand purchases have returned to favour with the spread of charity shops and boot sales. Not all children have multiple outfits and shoes, or the latest toys, though most know from television what they 'should' have. Teenagers in some households will only get the 'right' clothes and shoes if they earn money towards their cost, or resort to stealing or dealing.

And of course, towards the end of the spectrum where resources are scarcest, households still exist where children's labour, or their greater independence, still helps to bridge the economic gap. Older children of working (especially single) parents start sooner to fend for themselves after school. The poorer the household the more there is for them to do. Like their late nineteenth-century counterparts, they get younger siblings off to school and collect and care for them afterwards. They take loads of washing to the laundrette, help with heavy bags from the supermarket, do household chores and perhaps work in a family restaurant or shop, or find paid part-time work. Like poor children a hundred years ago, they may be irregular in attendance at school, tired and hungry in class, behind with school work and likely to resist discipline. As a result, they are often seen in terms of social problems.

Compulsory school now, as when it was introduced, amplifies any dissonance between the needs of the family and the demands of society, between an ideal of sheltered, dependent childhood and a reality of poverty and stress where children's help is indispensable. The label 'latchkey children', like fears that children watch too much television (or the wrong, adult, programmes), distils the anxiety of adults who want children to be more child-like, to have less responsibility and less autonomy, to conform with expectations of childhood which are now dominant in Britain and which cut across differences of class and of cultural background. At the same time, adults who do put domestic need before school requirements and child leisure are more likely to feel guilty, and their children may be more resentful of demands which are no longer 'normal'. Such tensions increase the probability of violence, threatened or actual, being used to enforce obedience, and this again invites stigma and state intervention. But intervention intended to keep teenagers within the family unit, the withdrawal of benefit for 16- to 18-year-olds, has created instead a street population of homeless teenagers supporting themselves by casual work, hassling, prostitution, begging or selling the *Big Issue*.

'What is a child?'

Although adult and child seem easy to identify through their difference and through the power relationship, the distinction between them is not simple. It is complicated by the diversity of possible positions and relationships within each group and by the extended transition from one status to the other.

The duration of childish dependence and subordination is not fixed, and neither is the content of the age role, for child or adult. Where religion is seen as central in adult life, it will dominate in the training of children; where the preoccupation is with work, or health or citizenship, those will feature more strongly.[38] What is seen as appropriate, at what age, for which children, varies between societies and also within them and over time. Conventions based on gender difference intersect with assumptions about age, and operate within social and economic structures, so that much also depends on the specific situation of child and adult. Historically as today ethnic background can also complicate both subjective and objective experience. A child growing up in a late nineteenth-century Irish or Jewish family in London would have experiences which distinguished her from neighbouring children, as well as ones in common.

The existence and character of the adolescent transition is similarly contingent. In the no-man's-land of adolescence, that stretch of years in the teens when the young may be fully grown but not yet adult, definitions are contested: 'You're not old enough' versus 'Don't treat me like a child'. And adult superiority may become less confident in these years: as children get bigger, physical coercion loses its force. Oral history and memoirs alike suggest that both in school and at home the use of corporal punishment often tailed off when the risk of retaliation became too great.

A child is someone at a certain stage in the life cycle. But that stage is open to different definitions, which in turn are open to challenge. It is not surprising, given the power relationship between adults and children, that children, in the course of growing up, will challenge adult definitions. What is interesting is that there is also often conflict between different adult interests, especially perhaps during periods of rapid change.

Ultimately childhood can only be defined in relative terms. The question 'What is a child?' must be followed by further questions – in whose eyes? When? Where? What are the implications?

Notes

1   This is documented by agencies like UNICEF and the International Labour Organisation. See also *Development and Change*, 13:4 (1982), issue on child labour. A recent estimate suggests some 200 million 'children under 15' currently working world-wide (Owen Bowcott, *Guardian*, 11 October 1987, p. 5), but this relatively high age ceiling again raises the question how far absolute definitions are possible.

2   See Maxine Berg, *The Age of Manufactures 1700–1820* (London, Fontana Paperbacks, 1984), ch. 6.

3   Peter Coveney, *The Image of Childhood: The Individual and Society: A Study of the Theme in English Literature* (London, Harmondsworth, [*Poor Monkey*, 1957] 1967); Hugh Cunningham, *The Children of the Poor: Representations of Childhood since the Seventeenth* Century (Oxford, Blackwell, 1991); Carolyn Steedman, *Childhood Culture and Class in Britain: Margaret McMillan 1860–1931* (London, Virago, 1990); Carolyn Steedman, *Strange Dislocations: Childhood and the Idea of Human Interiority 1780–1930* (London, Virago, 1995).

4   See Ellen Ross, *Love and Toil: Motherhood in Outcast London 1870–1918* (New York and Oxford, Oxford University Press, 1993), ch. 7.

5   See Frank Musgrove, *Youth and the Social Order* (Bloomington, Indiana University Press, 1964).

6   Anna Davin, *Growing Up Poor: Home, School and Street in London, 1870–1914* (London, Rivers Oram Press, 1996).

7   Sarah Boseley *The Guardian*, 13 March 1997, based on a report from the Office of National Statistics. The annual rate has been

consistently over 7,000 since at least 1970.

8 See Leonore Davidoff, 'Mastered for Life: Servant and Wife in Victorian and Edwardian England', in her *Worlds Between: Historical Perspectives on Gender and Class* (London, Polity Press, 1995).

9 Hannah More, *Coelebs in Search of a Wife* ([1809], Collected Works, London, 1830), p. 252.

10 William Makepeace Thackeray, *Vanity Fair* (London, 1847), ch. 1.

11 Leonore Davidoff and Catherine Hall, *Family Fortunes: Men and Women of the English Middle Class 1780–1850* (London, Hutchinson, 1987).

12 Eric Hopkins, *Childhood Transformed: Working-Class Children in Nineteenth-Century England* (Manchester, Manchester University Press, 1994); Davin, *Growing Up Poor*.

13 Gilbert James French, *The Life and Times of Samuel Crompton, Inventor of the Spinning Machine called the Mule* (Manchester, 1859), pp. 58–9.

14 William Hutton (ed. Catherine Hutton), *Life of William Hutton* (London, 1816), p. 12.

15 'Sketches in the Life of John Clare', in Eric Robinson (ed.), *John Clare's Autobiographical Writings* (Oxford, Oxford University Press, 1993), p. 3.

16 See for instance George Acorn's dramatic account (*One of the Multitude* [London, Heinemann, 1911], pp. 40–1) of carrying water upstairs for his mother in a heavy stone jar, and on the third trip, exhausted, falling 'down the whole flight of stairs into the passage to lie stunned amid the wreckage of the bottle and the sea of water which flooded the place'. A beating followed.

17 Henry Mayhew, *London Labour and the London Poor* (4 volumes, London, 1861–62), vol. I, pp. 151–2.

18 'Memories of Seventy Years, by Mrs Layton', in Margaret Llewelyn Davies (ed.), *Life as We have Known It by Co-operative Working Women* (London, Virago, [1931] 1977), pp. 20–1.

19 See the fictional Charley Neckett in Charles Dickens's *Bleak House* (1852–53), who took charge at thirteen when her mother died in childbed, then on her father's death went out washing and cleaning, helped by neighbours who kept an eye on the two little ones and found her jobs. Dickens combines admiration with a strong sense of wrong that responsibility and work should be shouldered by such a child: the word 'little' recurs constantly.

20 Mayhew, *London Labour*, I, p. 151.
21 Acorn, *One of the Multitude*, p. 69.
22 Seth Koven, 'Borderlands: Women, Voluntary Action, and Child Welfare in Britain, 1840–1914', in Seth Koven and Sonya Michel (eds), *Mothers of a New World: Maternalist Politics and the Origins of Welfare States* (New York and London, Routledge, 1993).
23 See Lyndal Roper, 'Blood and Codpieces: Masculinity in the Early Modern German Town', in her *Oedipus and the Devil: Witchcraft, Sexuality and Religion in Early Modern Europe* (London, Routledge, 1994), pp. 107–9.
24 Conrad Arensberg, *The Irish Countryman* (London, Macmillan, 1937), p. 131; ch. 4, 'Boys and Men'.
25 This was so even after the 1884 Reform Act. E. H. Hunt, *British Labour History 1815–1914* (London, Weidenfeld & Nicholson, 1981), p. 272 n.
26 Frances Hodgson Burnett, *A Little Princess* (London, Puffin, [1905] 1966), p. 67.
27 Samuel Butler, *The Way of All Flesh* (Jonathan Cape, [1903] 1932), pp. 26–7.
28 Will Crooks, *From Workhouse to Westminster: The Life of Will Crooks MP* (London, 1907), p. 6.
29 Jane Walsh, *Not Like This* (London, Lawrence and Wishart, 1953), p. 19.
30 Cécile de Banke's mother and aunt, for instance: *Hand over Hand* (London, Hutchinson, 1957), p. 51.
31 Paul Thompson, 'The War against Adults', *Oral History*, 3:2 (1975), 29–30.
32 See Mayhew, *London Labour*, I, p. 468; *Oxford English Dictionary* (by mid-century a 'child' was defined as 'a young person of either sex below the age of puberty'); Sykes, 'Hygiene and Sanitation in the Home and at School', in William Chance (ed.), *Proceedings of the Third International Conference for the Welfare and Protection of Children* (London, 1902), p. 26. The 1871 census (*Report*, p. xii) gave the 'stages of life' as children (5 to 9), boys and girls (10 to 14), and youths and maidens (15 to 19); its tables often make 20 a watershed. Puberty by 1883 was said to occur for boys between 14 and 16; for girls between 13 and 16: Crichton Browne, 'Education and the Nervous System', in Malcolm A. Morris (ed.), *The Book of Health* (London, 1883), p. 322.
33 For chronology (mainly for boys) see W. Clarke Hall, intro.

Benjamin Waugh, *The Queen's Reign for Children* (London, 1897), pp. 89–104; cf. Stanley B. Atkinson, 'Law and Infant Life', in Theophilus Kelynack (ed.), *Infancy* (London, 1910); Ivy Pinchbeck and Margaret Hewitt, *Children in English Society*, vol. II (London, Routledge and Kegan Paul, 1973), ch. 16; Thomas Alfred Spalding and T. S. A. Canney, *The Work of the London School Board* (London, 1900), pp. 137–46; Margaret May, 'Innocence and Experience: The Evolution of the Concept of Juvenile Delinquency in the Mid-Nineteenth Century', *Victorian Studies*, 17:1 (1973), pp. 7–23. The age of criminal responsibility was raised to 8 in 1933 and to 10 in 1963. The issue is again under debate.

34 Livius, *Father Furniss and his Work for Children* (London, 1896), pp. 137–8.

35 PRO, HO45 9764, Bridges to Lushington (both were London magistrates), 11 March 1893, cited in Charles K. Behlmer, *Child Abuse and Moral Reform in England 1870–1908* (Stanford, Stanford University Press, 1982), p. 158.

36 Deborah Gorham, '"The Maiden Tribute of Modern Babylon" Re-examined: Child Prostitution and the Idea of Childhood in late Victorian England', *Victorian Studies*, 21:3 (spring 1978) pp. 354–79; Jeffrey Weeks, *Sex, Politics and Society: The Regulation of Sexuality since 1800* (London, Longman, 1981), ch. 5; Frank Mort, *Dangerous Sexualities: Medico-Moral Politics in England since 1830* (London, Routledge and Kegan Paul, 1987), Part 3; Anna Davin, 'When is a Child not a Child?', in Lynn Jamieson and Helen Corr (eds), *Politics of Everyday Life* (London, Macmillan, 1990).

37 Ragged schools began in the 1840s, peaked in the 1860s, declined with school-board competition in the 1870s, picked up in the 1880s through extending their mission and charitable operations, and slumped in the 1890s with the abolition (in London) of school fees. The last one closed in 1906: see E. A. G. Clark, 'The Early Ragged Schools and the Foundation of the Ragged School Movement', *Journal of Educational Administration and History*, 1:2 (1969), pp. 9–21; 'The Last of the Voluntarists: The Ragged School Union in the School Board Era', *History of Education*, 11:1 (1982) pp. 23–4. The Ragged School Museum in London is at 46–50 Copperfield Rd, London E3 4RR.

38 See, for example, the Government's new scheme to teach citizenship in schools.

Death in childhood: the practice of the 'good death' in James Janeway's *A Token for Children*

'Did you never hear of a little Child that died? and if other Children die, why may not you be sick and die? and what will you do then, Child, if you should have no grace in your heart, and be found like other naughty Children?' Thus James Janeway addressed his imagined young readers in the preface to his *A Token for Children: being An Exact Account of the Conversion, Holy and Exemplary Lives, and Joyful Deaths, of several young Children*, entered in the Stationers' Register in 1671.[1] Janeway, a nonconformist minister, had been born in 1636 at Lilley (Hertfordshire), where his father had been curate. After studying at Christ Church, Oxford, he graduated B.A. in 1659. When he entered the ministry is uncertain. But he devoted himself to pastoral work in London during 1665, the last great plague year. A meeting house was later built for him in Rotherhithe.[2]

Janeway published a biography of his brilliant elder brother John (1633–57), in which he described how John, then only twenty, had supported their father William when the latter approached death. 'O Son!', William had confided in him, 'this passing upon eternity is a great thing, this dying is a solemn business and enough to make any ones heart ake, that hath not his pardon sealed, and his evidences for Heaven clear.' William told John how anxious he was about his own state. John went away and wrestled with God in prayer for his father, and William soon afterwards experienced a 'fit of overpowering love and joy'. John himself, his fragile health prematurely broken by overwork, allegedly experienced prolonged periods of almost inexpressible ecstasy while dying of consumption in 1657, crying out that death was sweet to him. He urged his mother to give him up to Christ. Before James in turn died of consumption in 1674, at the age of thirty-seven, he felt himself powerfully assaulted by Satan, who accused him of hypocrisy. But towards the end he blessed God for the assurance of his love, and broke into repeated hallelujahs, full of grateful praise for redemption by free grace.[3]

James's intense experience of the spectacle of death in his own family establishes part of the context necessary for the understanding of his *Token*. His dying father and brother had felt an assurance of God's love which they had communicated to those around them. Janeway believed quite young children capable of deaths like theirs, and death-bed victories crown most of the lives recounted in his *Token*, taking up the greater part of many of the narratives. Janeway was not the first narrator of godly children's deaths. He included three previously published narratives in his own collection. The description of one boy's experiences came from a work by Isaac Ambrose (1604–63), a Lancashire Presbyterian minister, and the lives of two other children had first been published in Dutch. The story of the exemplary life of Caleb Vernon (1666) may have seemed too long to use. Another author, Thomas White, published *A Little Book for Little Children*, which included not only several directions for such children, but also stories of children both ancient and modern, some of whom had died recently. Janeway recommended White's book to children in one of the prefaces to his own work.[4]

The two parts of Janeway's *Token* include thirteen lives. The deaths of eight of the children are dated. One, the earliest, had occurred in 1632, two in the 1640s, four in 1664–65, and the most recent in 1671. Nine of the thirteen children were named. For the majority of his cases, Janeway probably relied on the testimony of friends and acquaintances. The children's social status was seldom precisely specified, but their backgrounds clearly varied. The most easily identified of all the parents was John Bridgeman, bishop of Chester, whose son Charles's life story had been told by Isaac Ambrose.[5] Among the other fathers were a minister, a merchant, and a man who had kept a shop. Two of the children were described as poor, and one of these had been a beggar until taken in by a benefactor. Many of Janeway's accounts supply the reader with little information about the chil-

dren's parents. In some cases, both parents were alive at the time
of the child's death. One child had already lost her father, and
two had probably lost both parents.[6] In some cases parents play
so small a part in the story that it is impossible to tell whether
they were alive or dead. Apart from the Dutch children and
Charles Bridgeman, most of the individuals whose experiences
Janeway described had probably lived in or near London. Three
of them were born into families resident in Middlesex, Kent, and
Colnbrook (Buckinghamshire) respectively.[7] Seven of the thirteen
children were boys and six girls. Most important of all for the
purposes of the analysis which follows are the ages of the children
at death. The eldest, Sarah Howley, was at least 14, and the
Dutch girl Susanna Bicks was 13. Of the remaining children, three
were 12 or thereabouts, one 11, two 9, one 8, one 7, and one 5
or 6.[8] In sum: the children who appear in Janeway's collection
had been born into a variety of social groups, ranging from the
higher clergy to the very poor, represented both sexes almost
equally, and died for the most part in later childhood not long
before he wrote.

Infant and child mortality were far heavier in later seventeenth-
century England than they are today. In provincial England,
about three out of ten children born may have died before the age
of fifteen. Yet well over half of these deaths occurred during the
first year of life: infant mortality stood at just under 170 per
1,000 between 1650 and 1699. Mortality fell sharply after
infancy: the corresponding rates for the age groups 1–4, 5–9, and
10–14, were 101.5, 40, and 24.2. The situation in London was a
good deal worse, and worst of all in the poorest parishes. In the
wealthy parish of St Peter Cornhill, between 1580 and 1650, just
over a third of the children born had probably died before the age
of ten. In a poor parish, St Mary Somerset, between 1605 and
1653, the corresponding proportion was almost exactly a half.
During the later seventeenth century the metropolitan infant
mortality rate was probably over 333.33 per 1,000. Yet even in
London a child of five had a fairly good prospect of surviving till
at least the age of fifteen. Death during the periods of childhood
with which Janeway was most concerned was the lot of a small
minority. Indeed, fewer individuals died between the ages of ten
and fifteen than at any other stage of life before old age. But the
mortality patterns outlined above changed dramatically during

outbreaks of plague. The proportions of people buried in the
5–19 age group was at least twice the norm during some major
epidemics, and in three London parishes approached 50 per cent
of all burials in 1593. Paul Slack comments that 'no other age-
group appears to have suffered so disproportionately'. It is
significant that at least four of the thirteen children whose stories
Janeway told died during the plagues of 1664 (in Holland) and
1665 (in London). In most of the other cases he did not identify
the nature of the terminal illness.[9]

The essential foundation for the sort of good death described
by Janeway was personal religious awareness. Such awareness
had developed in several of these children some years before their
deaths, most often between four and six. One unnamed boy was
said to have been 'admirably affected with the things of God,
when he was between two and three years old' and to have cried
after God before he could speak plainly, but he was exceptional.
Parents not surprisingly played the key part in some of the children's early religious development. The mother of the last
mentioned boy dedicated him to God while he was still in the
womb. The parents of another boy tried to instill spiritual princi-
ples into him as soon as he was capable of understanding them,
and his mother supervised the education of a third. But sources of
instruction outside the family were also important: schools in a
number of cases, and sermons in one, or possibly two. Sarah
Howley (d. 1671) was 'awakened' by the exposition of Matthew
11: 30. Mary A. was greatly affected by hearing the Word of God.
(Several of the children experienced some sort of conversion or
awakening, but Janeway's references to these experiences are
usually relatively brief.)[10]

A remarkable feature of several of the stories told by Janeway
is the early development of a degree of autonomy. Several children read and prayed by themselves. Various boys and girls tried
to 'awaken' other children, rebuked them, or taught them to pray.
The most precocious of the thirteen could not endure being put to
bed before family duty (prayers, perhaps also a reading from
scripture) had been performed, and reminded his parents of it.
Anne Lane, eminently religious before the age of six, prompted
her father's conversion with her concern for his soul. Watchful of
her parents' behaviour, she was sad to see her father in unprof-
itable company, and reminded him of the preciousness of time

'with much sweetness and humility'. According to Janeway, John Harvy never disputed his parents' commands *except* when he thought them contrary to God's.[11]

Over half the English children were described as keenly interested in their fate after death, and in some cases anxious about it. John Sudlow was about four when a little brother of his died. Seeing the lifeless child put into a pit-hole, John 'was greatly concerned, and asked notable questions about him'. Being told that he too must die 'made such a deep impression upon him, that from that time forward he was exceeding serious'. To know what to do in order to avoid dying for ever became a major concern of his. One four-year-old, Mary A., greatly affected by hearing the Word of God, became very concerned about her soul, 'weeping bitterly to think what would become of her in another world'. She often wondered how she would spend her time in the next life, and asked, 'O what are they doing which are already in Heaven?' In the case of Tabitha Alder, daughter of a 'holy and reverend' minister in Kent, an illness which she suffered at the age of seven was the catalyst for fears that she was destined for hell because she did not love God. (It seems entirely natural that she found it hard to love someone she couldn't see.) The youngest child, who died at five or six, found it very strange to think that 'the same weak body that was buried in the Church-yard, should be raised again'.[12]

Some of these children assimilated so effectively what they were taught that they were able to reinforce the faith of adults. When John Harvy was not yet five, his mother was greatly troubled by her brother's death. John reminded her that it would not be long before the last judgement, when they would see each other again. Her sorrow for her brother turned into wonder at her child, and she sat quietly under the 'smarting stroke' of her loss. After her father's death Mary A. consoled her mother, telling her that she had no cause to weep so much, for God was still a good God to her.[13]

Nearly all these children allegedly died in a state of cheerful confidence. But, not surprisingly, these happy ends were sometimes preceded by periods of more or less acute anxiety. The story of Sarah Howley, the oldest of the children (d. 1671), contains a vivid account of the vicissitudes of death-bed moods. Despite her previous industry, obedience, and religious reading, she was oppressed by a very strong sense of sin and a fear of damnation. At one point she urged her mother to pray on her behalf, saying that Satan was so busy that she couldn't pray for herself. (A complaint similar to Sarah's had been made by at least one other dying puritan heroine, Katherine Brettergh [d. 1601], whose life story Sarah might have read.) Mary A. was also involved, shortly before her death, in a conflict with Satan, which caused her to cry out that she was none of his.[14]

The former beggar boy's spiritual ordeal was the most protracted. Before being taken in by a kind friend of Janeway's, he had 'by the corruption of his Nature, and the abominable example of little beggar boyes ... arrived to a strange pitch of impiety'. On the onset of his final illness, when he was nine, this boy found his former sins staring him in the face, and suffered terrible agonies of spirit along with a sense of God's wrath: he feared that he would go to hell and that there was no hope for him. The growing awareness of a 'natural' self and an 'ideal' self is a normal part of the child's development. This sense of two identities was perhaps heightened in the beggar boy's case. He had been subjected to contradictory pressures by the two sharply contrasting social environments to which he had had to adapt, and the torment which he suffered during his final illness might be envisaged as the result of an unresolved conflict between the two personalities which had been necessary for survival in two very different milieux. The youngest child, dying at the age of five or six after spending his short life in the bosom of a religious family, quite quickly overcame the fears about his state in another world which assailed him when he first fell ill. Not long afterwards, asked whether he was willing to die, he answered that he was, because he would be going to Christ.[15]

Some of the children underwent an ecstatic experience. Three days before Sarah Howley died, when everybody thought she was past speaking, she broke out into rapturous praise. God would not cast her out. 'O so sweet! O so glorious is Jesus! O I have the sweet and glorious Jesus: he is sweet, he is sweet, he is sweet! O the admirable love of God in sending Christ! O free grace to a poor lost Creature!' Many of these things she repeated a hundred times over. Sarah may have been consumptive, and her experience somewhat resembled Janeway's own. Several of the children experienced a vision of glory, or of angelic messengers who would shortly take them to heaven, and two of them accurately predicted the day of their death some time beforehand. To the converted beggar boy the angels appeared as 'brave Gentlemen'. Mary A. felt a great sense of God's love, and saw a glorious sight, 'as if she had seen the very Heavens open, and the Angels come to receive her'.[16]

Some of the dying children are described as receiving support and encouragement from family, friends, and godly ministers. Sarah Howley, unlike some of the other children in Janeway's collection, lived in the heart of a sizeable family which included both parents, brothers, and sisters and a grandmother. The household also included a number of servants. She was visited by a young kinsman and some ministers. Her mother appears to have been Sarah's chief spiritual confidante. Her father tried to encourage her, saying that she was going to a better Father, although she responded by vehemently lamenting her want of assurance. The visiting ministers begged God to give her some encouraging sign, so that 'she might go off triumphing', and requests for prayers to the same effect were sent to several churches. Of all the individuals whose experiences were described, it was the Dutch children, Susanna and Jacob Bicks, who appear to have received the most sustained support from their parents in the form of both spiritual encouragement and expressions of affection. Janeway wrote relatively little about the help given by the parents of most of the English children, training his spotlight on the dying individual and seeking above all to illustrate the working of God's grace rather than the social or familial context of the death bed. It was probably the unnamed beggar boy who benefited most from spiritual advice. The man sent by God to take care of his soul reminded the boy that Christ came to seek and save sinners. A godly friend of Janeway's removed the boy's last fears, on the day before his death, by assuring him that Christ was a thousand times more willing to have him, wash him, and save him, than he was to desire it. Some of the children were asked whether they were willing to die. The question seems a somewhat chilling one to modern sensibilities. It gave the strong an opportunity of declaring their faith, and the weak of disclosing their fears or misapprehensions so that they might be counselled or comforted as the beggar boy was. It elicited some fairly robust expressions of confidence as well as admissions of anxiety.[17]

One reason for asking a child whether he was ready to die was the questioner's own need for reassurance. This emerges very clearly from the account of conversations between the eleven-year-old John Harvy and his mother. Their house was visited by the plague in 1665. His sister had already died, and his brother was marked not long after John fell sick. He asked his mother to pray for him. She answered that she was so full of grief that she could not pray, but she wanted to hear him say his last prayer. It was at this point that she asked him whether he was willing to die and leave her. He replied that he was, and to go to his heavenly Father. She answered, 'Child, If thou hadst but an assurance of Gods love I should not be so much troubled.' John told her that he was assured that his sins were forgiven and that he would go to heaven. When his mother burst into tears, he said that she would not weep but rejoice if she knew what joy he felt. In an effort to divert her, he asked her, trying (we might think) to strike a note of homely normality, what she had had for supper. He shortly cried out, 'O what a sweet Supper have I making ready for me in glory.' Finally, seeing that his words only increased his mother's grief, he called on her to humble herself under God's hand.[18]

This was an extreme example of the reversal of roles which sometimes appears to have taken place at the death beds of these children, whose early deaths and precocious piety put them in the position of acting a part more naturally fulfilled by dying parents towards their children. But it was not unique. Mary A., who fell sick at about the same age as John Harvy, did her best with arguments from scripture 'to support and encourage her Relations to part with her that was going to Glory, and to prepare themselves to meet her in a blessed Eternity'. Her mother told Mary she was sorry she had so often reproved and corrected so good a child. Mary answered that she blessed God for her mother's reproofs and corrections, without which she might have gone to hell. Sarah Howley prayed that God would support and comfort her mother, who was still grieving for a recently dead son. They would, she hoped, shortly meet in Glory. Susanna Bicks, active in trying to comfort her family, looked forward to the resurrection, and, more immediately, to reunion with a younger brother and sister who had predeceased her.[19]

Besides imparting a comforting sense of their own hopes or

assurance to those around them, godly adults often gave good advice about the performance of Christian duties before they died. Parents in particular were expected to do so. It is hardly surprising that the giving of such advice is not a very prominent theme of Janeway's narratives. But Sarah Howley, the oldest child, poured out urgent exhortations, especially to other young people. She gave her Bible as her legacy to one of her brothers, asking him to use it well for her sake. The twelve-year-old Mary A. told some visiting neighbours that if they served the Lord they would follow her to glory.[20]

The cases assembled by Janeway in the two parts of his work were unusual ones. He himself referred to them as 'God's works of Wonder' in the Preface addressed to adults at the beginning of the first part. He felt bound to assure his readers that his accounts rested on completely reliable testimony or his own knowledge. He nevertheless admitted in the Preface to the second part that his story of the child who had begun to be serious between two and three had encountered incredulity even among the godly. His principal authority for this story was a Mrs Jeofries of Bermondsey, a woman of such a high reputation that her testimony was of almost as much authority as that of any minister. Two men, a godly gentleman out of the country, and the famous puritan hagiographer Samuel Clarke, had described similar cases. 'What is too hard for the Almighty?', he concluded. 'Hath God said he will work no more wonders?'[21] But Janeway seems not to have thought any such vigorous defence necessary in the case of the older children who appeared in his collection. Presumably their stories did not encounter as much scepticism as the account of the youngest and most precocious boy.

Janeway's judgements of individual children were based on descriptions of their capacities and behaviour. The age which they had reached had no independent significance for him. The great majority of the children whose ages are given were nevertheless older than seven, as has already been remarked, even though their godly inclinations had in most cases begun to manifest themselves in earlier childhood. The age of seven, the boundary between early and later childhood in one widely accepted medieval scheme, is still recognised today as an important stage in child development. Janeway's cases do not lend themselves to systematic analysis within the frameworks set by modern studies of child

psychology.[22] But a broad developmental progression is nevertheless apparent among them, its stages very roughly
corresponding with the children's ages at death. It was the oldest
children, in general, who showed the greatest spiritual autonomy
and capacity to emulate the best models of godly dying, seeking
to comfort those around them. Apart from the beggar boy (who
died at the age of nine), a somewhat exceptional case, it was two
of the older children, including the oldest, Sarah Howley, who
were recorded as experiencing the strongest sense of Satanic
temptation before their happy ends. Two of the children, including the youngest, reportedly had difficulty in assimilating certain
religious beliefs or concepts.[23] Certainly many of these accounts
share certain common elements, but there are also significant
differences between them, and these differences enhance their
credibility.

Janeway wrote a relatively slender account of the only death
recorded in his collection which occurred before the age of seven.
Yet one very full and vivid private narrative of a young child's
death bed survives, written only thirteen years before the publication of the first part of Janeway's compilation. The fact that it
was the product of a completely different religious milieu from
Janeway's gives it an added interest. John Evelyn, a devout and
learned supporter of the Church of England in its pre-revolution-
ary form, was immensely proud of his exceptionally precocious
son Richard, who died at the age of five in 1658. Richard had
already made substantial progress in Latin and French, had a
'strange passion for Greeke' and a 'wonderfull disposition to
Mathematics', and showed a restless intellectual curiosity. More
importantly, he had a remarkable if necessarily immature understanding of religion. He had learnt the whole catechism, and
understood not only the historical part of the Bible, but also how
Christ had come to redeem mankind. He had, his father remembered, 'declaim'd against the Vanities of the World, before he had
seene any', and had been able to give a coherent account of a
sermon he had just heard.[24]

During his sickness, Richard himself selected 'the most pathetical *Psalmes*, & Chapters out of Jobe' to read to his maid. When
she pitied him, he told her that all God's children must suffer
affliction. The day before he died, he called to his father, 'and in
a more serious manner than usualy' told Evelyn that he should

give his house, land, and all his fine things to his brother Jack. When he first felt ill, and his father tried to persuade him to keep his hands in bed, Richard asked whether he might pray to God with his hands unjoined, and a little later, in great agony, whether he would offend God by so often using his holy name in calling upon him for some relief from pain. He also uttered 'frequent pathetical ejaculations' such as 'Sweete *Jesus* save me, deliver me, pardon my sinns, Let thine *Angels* receive me &c'.[25]

John Evelyn thought several aspects of his son's behaviour remarkable. Perhaps the most striking elements in the narrative we have inherited are Richard's seeming understanding and acceptance of the approach of death, evident both in his foreseeing that he would not inherit his father's property and in his final prayers. If Richard was afraid to die, there is no evidence of it in his father's account. Neither he in his recorded utterances, nor his father, in his later comments on Richard's death, expressed anxiety about the destination of his soul. Richard Evelyn seems from his father's account to have been an outstanding example of some of the traits we might expect to find in a precocious child of his age. On the one hand he had a well-established personality, a strong will, and a hunger for understanding. On the other hand his values and sense of identity had been shaped by his loving parents, and especially by his father. They had dominated his experience. One may speculate that his sense of security was founded on his father's approval and the as yet unbroken and unquestioned consistency and coherence of the universal picture which the elder Evelyn presented to his son. His parents could not protect him from death, but his mental and imaginative world was a sheltered one, untroubled by serious doubt or an acute sense of evil.

Children who were too young to be capable of even the most rudimentary religious understanding or to be able to communicate their thoughts and feelings in speech lacked the fundamental requisites of the 'good' death. Yet the diarist Alice Thornton, whose churchmanship was broadly similar to Evelyn's, seems to have sought to reassure herself that the outcome had been a happy one even when her children died very young. In 1656, her eighteen-month-old daughter Elizabeth endured a 'racking cough' with 'infinite patience', and then, when her parents came to pray for her, 'she held up those sweet eyes and hands to her dear Father in heaven, looked up, and cried in her language, "Dad, dad, dad", with such vehemency as if inspired by her holy Father in heaven to deliver her sweet soul into her heavenly Father's hands . . .', before falling asleep and dying 'like a lamb'. Alice's son William lived only eleven days after his birth in 1660, yet as he lay in her arms he 'would sweetly lift up his eyes to heaven and smile, as if the old saying was true in this sweet infant, that he saw angels in heaven'. Her only source of comfort when he died was her hope that God had received him into that place of rest in heaven where little children beheld the face of their heavenly father.[26]

These examples from the journals of John Evelyn and Alice Thornton show that it was possible for devout parents to discern elements of the good death in the last moments of children even younger than those whose experiences were recorded by Janeway. Several seventeenth-century diarists who wrote about their sons' or daughters' death beds do not however seem to have interpreted them as crowning triumphs of faith like those in which Janeway's narratives culminate. Even when children might be considered to have 'died well', their comportment was usually somewhat briefly described. In 1654 the royalist Lady Fanshawe and her husband lost their beloved eight-year-old daughter Ann, whom her mother described as the companion of their travels and sorrows. Her account of Ann's death was concise and comparatively reticent. 'She lay sick but five days of the small-pox; in which time she expressed many wise and devout sayings, as is a miracle for her years.' The Suffolk clergyman Isaac Archer tried to counsel his five-year-old daughter on her death bed in 1679 but his efforts seem to have been only partially successful. He started to catechise her, but she got no further than telling him that God had made her, because speaking was painful. He next asked her 'if she would goe to God', but though she looked earnestly on him, she said nothing. Archer nevertheless assured her that she was going to heaven to her brothers and sisters, and that they would all meet again. When the puritan minister Ralph Josselin lost his eight-year-old daughter Mary in 1650, he recorded no attempt to prepare her spiritually for her impending departure, and included no devout sayings or prayers of hers in the daily diary entries which he made for the final week of her life. Her last recorded utterance, just under three days before the end, concerned her hopes of relief from the distressing physical symptoms of her disease, rather than preparation for an imminent departure. Yet when she finally died, Josselin described her as falling asleep in the Lord: her soul, he confidently wrote, had passed into that rest where the body of Jesus and the souls of the saints were. This was a judgement based less on the manner of her death than on the promise of her life, for she had been 'a child of ten thousand, full of wisedome, woman-like gravity, knowledge, sweet expressions of god, apt in her learning, tender hearted and loving' as well as obedient to her parents.[27]

A number of parents consoled themselves with the reflection that heavenly bliss awaited the souls of innocent children. Nehemiah Wallington, a godly London wood turner, lost all except one of his five children in early childhood between 1625 and 1632. He was distraught when he lost during the plague of 1625 his three-year-old daughter Elizabeth, whose playfully affectionate last words he carefully recorded. It was his wife who consoled Wallington for the loss of two of their children, including Elizabeth, reminding him of their heavenly happiness with a seemingly unquestioning faith. When Ralph Josselin lost his baby son Ralph ten days after his birth in 1648, he felt certain that he would witness his child's resurrection. (Josselin, while not questioning his infant son's salvation, thought that God must have intended to correct his own faults by taking the child away. Isaac Archer, who lost all but one of his nine children, responded to some of their deaths in a similar fashion, though after his eighth loss he found it very hard to understand why God was punishing him so severely.)[28]

The reality of heaven and the next life in the imaginations of some early modern children is illustrated by a number of diaries and autobiographies. In an exceptionally vivid dream recorded by his father in 1654 Ralph Josselin's son Tom was drawn up into heaven by Jesus Christ. He found the inhabitants 'singing melodiously and praying all in white' and met his sister Mary, who had died four years before. She tried to detain him in heaven, but Jesus insisted that he must leave. In this ten-year-old boy's dream, Christ appeared as a powerful but loving figure who openly confirmed his close relationship with Tom's earthly father by hugging Ralph Josselin in the pulpit. Alice Thornton wrote two strikingly similar accounts of attempts by one of her children, each of them aged six at the time, to console her after a death in the family. In both cases they reminded her of the happiness which the recently departed (Alice's husband, and a baby son) were enjoying in heaven. Did she want them to leave this happy state? None but the spirit of God could put such words into the mouth of a child only six years and four months old, Alice reflected after her son Robert's attempt to comfort her on her husband's death in 1668. An even younger child for whom heaven appears to have been a powerful imagined reality was Mary (1654–58), three-year-old daughter of the Lancashire minister Adam Martindale. A very clever child for her age, she seemed 'utterly to despise life' after her little brother died in March 1657 when he was only three months old. She 'would frequently talke of heaven and being buried by him', and in this last point her wish was respected.[29]

Christian beliefs concerning the afterlife were, according to Janeway's account, among the most important formative influences on the children whose lives he described. Janeway believed that children were not too little to go to either heaven or hell. He unequivocally predicted that disobedient, truant, lying, children who spoke naughty words and broke the Sabbath were destined to suffer eternal punishment.[30] In a miserable condition by nature, the inheritors of original sin, children were not incapable of receiving the grace of God. Before the Reformation, the Roman Catholic Church had held the baptised infant incapable of mortal sin until the age of discretion, conventionally placed around the end of the seventh year. Several of the Protestant reformers attributed less power to the rite of baptism and took a less sanguine view of childish innocence.[31] In fact nearly all the children in Janeway's collection were seven or older when they died, but it was possible for children younger than seven to be precociously bad, just as the youngest boy in *A Token* was precociously good.

Janeway was actuated by an urgent desire to save souls, to him the all-important pastoral responsibility. His commitment to the salvation of children's souls might be compared with that of more modern reformers to the saving of their lives through improved sanitation, nutrition, and working conditions.

> His bowels of compassion yearned towards immortal souls. He knew the worth of his own and the souls of others, and as he was acquainted with the value of souls, so he was sensible of their

danger. How earnestly would he warn them to flee from future wrath? ... He pitied the souls of all, old, young; nay he was deeply concerned for little Children, witness those books which he styles *tokens* for them.[32]

Some modern commentators, lacking the religious convictions and urgent concerns of Janeway and other 'puritan' writers for children, have commented harshly on their work. Sandford Fleming, author of *Children and Puritanism,* remarked that some of Janeway's stories 'tax one's credulity'. He criticised the Puritans' failure to recognize children's needs and the Puritan demand for an abnormal religious experience on the part of children, in which an appeal to fear played an unhealthy part.[33] Gordon Rattray Taylor thought Janeway's books 'horrifying'.[34] By no means all commentators have been equally hostile. Professor C. John Sommerville has turned on its head the charge that Janeway was insensitive to the needs and aptitudes of children, praising his readiness to take them seriously and address them directly.[35] In fact the children whose stories Janeway recounted do not for the most part appear to have been subjected to the 'fantastic pressures' condemned by Gordon Rattray Taylor. They responded to influences present in their intellectual environment in a way which surprised many of those closest to them. Their exceptional religious precocity gave some of them a degree of independence in the face of parental authority.

This chapter has attempted a sympathetic appraisal of one facet of Janeway: that of narrator of exemplary deaths. His *Token* was informed by the conviction that children were not too young to be damned. The next life was infinitely more important than the transitory existence on earth, yet it was by their actions in the latter that the eternal fate of individuals was determined. A happy death, in which the dying person communicated a powerful sense of God's love to spectators, was a fitting crown of a good life. Were children capable of such a death? Janeway answered unequivocally that they were. Some of the narratives illustrating this proposition encountered disbelief. Yet the corpus contains many highly realistic and convincing details. The children in Janeway's stories were portrayed as differing in maturity and understanding, as well as in their consciousness of sin. Some of them grappled with religious concepts which they found hard to

understand as well as with the shocking facts of death. Their
death-bed actions may have been unusual for individuals of their
age groups, even among the godly. But they lay at one end of a
spectrum of conventional behaviour, not in the realm of patho-
logical abnormality. Furthermore, although these stories contain
elements especially characteristic of the puritan *ars moriendi*,
interest in the death-bed comportment of children was certainly
not limited to puritans. Janeway's earliest narrative described the
last days of a bishop's son, and one of the fullest of all accounts
of a little boy's death bed was written by John Evelyn, a loyal son
of the Church of bishops and Prayer Book. The mental world
which Janeway inhabited seems utterly foreign from the stand-
point of the late twentieth century. The dramatic reduction of
infant and child mortality, and even more importantly the transformation and decline of religious belief, lie between him and us.
Yet his stories may still speak to us, not merely of fears we think
morbid or fantastic, but of human love and grief, of the anguish
of parting, and of hopes more potent than most of us now
possess.

Notes

1   J. Janeway, *A Token for Children: being An Exact Account of the
    Conversion, Holy and Exemplary Lives, and Joyful Deaths, of
    several young Children* (2 parts in 1 volume, London, 1676), unpag-
    inated preface containing directions to children. In this edition the
    second part is dated 1673. Yet *A token for children, the first and
    second p(ar)te*, by James Janeway, was entered in the Stationers'
    Register on 13 October 1671: *A Transcript of the Registers of the
    Worshipful Company of Stationers, from 1640–1708 A.D.*, ed. G.
    E. B. Eyre, H. R. Plomer and C. R. Rivington (3 vols, repr. New
    York, Peter Smith, 1950), II, p. 432. The first part appears in Wing
    (J477A) as published in Edinburgh in 1672.
2   *Dictionary of National Biography*; A. J. King, *Shining Faces: Five
    Generations of Janeways* (Royston, North Hertfordshire Villages
    Research Group, 1990), pp. 32–41, 61–8.
3   J. Janeway, *Invisibles, Realities, Demonstrated in the Holy Life and
    Triumphant Death of M$^{r.}$ John Janeway, Fellow of Kings Colledge
    in Cambridge* (London, 1673), pp. 100–2, 108, 113–14; N.
    Vincent, *The Saints Triumph over the Last Enemy. In a Sermon*

Preached at the Funeral of that Zealous and Painful Minister of Christ, Mr. James Janeway. Unto which is added, His Character. His sore Conflict before he dyed: And afterwards, His Triumphant manner of departing from Earth, to the Heavenly Inheritance (London, 1674), pp. 34–6.

4 Janeway, *Token*, I, pp. 43–9; II, pp. 23–64; I. Ambrose, *Prima, the First Things, In reference to the Middle & Last Things: Or, The Doctrine of Regeneration the New Birth, The very beginning of a Godly life*, in *The Compleat Works of that Eminent Minister of Gods Word Mr Isaac Ambrose* (London, 1674), pp. 380–2. According to Janeway, the account of the two Dutch children had first been translated into Scots. *An edifying wonder of two children, Susanna Bickes, also Jacob Bickes* was published at Glasgow in 1668: H. G. Aldis, *A List of Books printed in Scotland before 1700* (2nd edn, Edinburgh, National Library of Scotland, 1970), no. 1841.2. Wing lists under [Simpson, Mr.] an edition [n. p.] of 1666 (S3807A). Was its Scottish publication in some way connected with the Edinburgh edition of the first part of Janeway's *Token*? John Vernon's account of his son, *The Compleat Scholler; or, A Relation of the Life, and Latter-End especially, of Caleb Vernon; who dyed in the Lord on the 29th of the ninth month, 1665. Aged twelve years and six months. Commending to Youth the most Excellent Knowledge of Christ Jesus the Lord* (London, 1666), was partly inspired by concerns very close to Janeway's, and is very similar in tone to his lives. But the Vernons were Baptists, and there is nothing to show that any of Janeway's material had a Baptist provenance. White's *Little Book* was published as early as 1660, according to G. Avery, 'The Puritans and Their Heirs', in G. Avery and J. Briggs (eds), *Children and Their Books: A Celebration of the Work of Iona and Peter Opie* (Oxford, Clarendon Press, 1989), p. 117, n. 4. Avery's chapter and C. J. Somerville, *The Discovery of Childhood in Puritan England* (Athens and London, University of Georgia Press, 1992) are useful surveys of Puritan writing for children.

5 Janeway, *Token*, I, p. 43 (where John Bridgeman's office is not mentioned); H. Fishwick, *History of the Parish of Garstang in the County of Lancaster* (Chetham Society, old series 104–5, 1878–9), II, p. 162.

6 Janeway, *Token*, I, pp. 8–9, 28–9, 48, 50, 54, 56–7; II, pp. 12–13, 16, 19, 55–6, 62–3, 65.

7 *Ibid.*, II, pp. 1, 14, 19.

8   *Ibid.,* I, pp. 5, 26, 38, 43, 56; II, pp. 1, 18, 22, 60, 61, 83.
9   E. A. Wrigley and R. S. Schofield, 'English Population History from
     Family Reconstitution: Summary Results 1600–1799', *Population
     Studies,* 37:2 (1983), 177; R. A. P. Finlay, *Population and
     Metropolis: The Demography of London, 1580–1650* (Cambridge,
     Cambridge University Press, 1981), p. 107; J. Landers, *Death and
     the Metropolis: Studies in the Demographic History of London,
     1670–1830* (Cambridge, Cambridge University Press, 1993), pp.
     98–101, 170; T. R. Forbes, 'By What Disease or Casualty: The
     Changing Face of Death in London', in C. Webster (ed.), *Health,
     Medicine and Mortality in the Sixteenth Century* (Cambridge,
     Cambridge University Press, 1979), p. 124; P. Slack, *The Impact of
     Plague in Tudor and Stuart England* (Oxford, Clarendon Press,
     1985), pp. 181–2; Janeway, *Token,* I, pp. 5, 10–12, 36; II, pp. 25,
     61, 83–4.
10   *Ibid.,* I, pp. 2–3, 19, 20, 27, 29, 41–2, 43–4; II, pp. 1, 65, 66, 67.
11   *Ibid.,* I, pp. 2–3, 19, 30, 40, 43, 45; II, 15–16, 69–70, 75–8.
12   *Ibid.,* I, pp. 2–3, 24–5, 27, 32–3; II, pp. 2–3, 19. Richard Norwood,
     recalling his 1590s childhood in his autobiography, remembered
     how his parents had seemed to smile at his childishness when 'taken
     with great admiration' (i.e. wonder) he drew their attention to St
     Paul's description of the resurrection in 1 Corinthians 15. 'Upon
     which and the like occasions I often doubted whether things were
     really so as I conceived them or whether elder people did not know
     them to be otherwise, only they were willing that we children should
     be so persuaded of them, that we might follow our books the better
     and be kept in from play.' See *The Journal of Richard Norwood,
     Surveyor of Bermuda,* ed. W. F. Craven and W. B. Hayward (New
     York, Scholars' Facsimiles and Reprints, 1945), p. 8.
13   Janeway, *Token,* I, pp. 28–9; II, pp. 66–7, 83.
14   *Ibid.,* I, pp. 4–7, 37; S. Clarke, *The Second part of the Marrow of
     Ecclesiastical History: Containing the Lives of Christians of
     Inferiour Ranks* (London, 1675), II, pp. 54–5.
15   Janeway, *Token,* I, pp. 25–6, 57–8, 61–6; J. A. Hadfield, *Childhood
     and Adolescence* (Penguin Books, Harmondsworth, 1962), pp.
     138–9.
16   Janeway, *Token,* I, pp. 12, 16, 18, 38, 47–8, 68; II, pp. 22, 59, 85.
17   *Ibid.,* I, pp. 6–16, 25, 46, 62–3, 69–70; II, pp. 13, 26–8, 31–3, 36–7,
     39–40, 49–50, 53, 56, 62–3.
18   *Ibid.,* II, pp. 83–7.

19   *Ibid.,* I, pp. 9–10, 35–7; II, pp. 32–6, 40–1, 52–4, 62–3.

20   W. Perkins, *A Salve for a Sicke Man: or, a Treatise containing the nature, differences, and kindes of death; as also the right manner of dying well* (London, edn of c. 1638), pp. 151–2; Janeway, *Token,* I, pp. 10, 13–15, 37.

21   *Ibid.,* I, sig. A5; II, sig. A2–A4.

22   *On the Properties of Things: John Trevisa's Translation of Bartholomaeus Anglicus 'De Proprietatibus Rerum'. A Critical Text,* ed. M. C. Seymour and others (3 vols, Oxford, Oxford University Press, 1975–88), I, pp. 291, 300; Hadfield, *Childhood and Adolescence,* pp. 159–79; J. Gabriel, *Children Growing Up: The Development of Children's Personalities* (London, University of London Press, 1964), pp. 186–99, 213–35; K. E. Hyde, *Religion in Childhood and Adolescence: A Comprehensive Review of the Research* (Birmingham, Ala., Religious Education Press, 1990), esp. pp. 15–34, 64–82, 383–91. The fact that there are only nine page references to 'heaven' and 'hell' in the index of this book (*ibid.,* p. 506), gives some impression of the difficulty of comparing the religious conceptions of twentieth-century children with those of seventeenth-century children. Cf. S. Anthony, *The Discovery of Death in Childhood and After* (Harmondsworth, Penguin, 1971), pp. 119–36.

23   Janeway, *Token,* I, p. 20; II, pp. 24–5.

24   *The Diary of John Evelyn,* ed. E. S. De Beer (6 vols, Oxford, Clarendon Press, 1955), III, pp. 206–9.

25   *Ibid.,* p. 208. For a story of a four-year-old boy's giving everything he had to his brother, see G. Holles, *Memorials of the Holles Family 1493–1656,* ed. A. G Wood (Camden 3rd series, 55, 1937), p. 195. This child, John Holles, was thought 'likely in all probability (excepting his over forwardnes) to have lived many yeares'.

26   *The Autobiography of Mrs Alice Thornton of East Newton, Co. York,* ed. C. Jackson (Surtees Society, 62, 1875 for 1873), pp. 94, 124–5.

27   *The Memoirs of Ann Lady Fanshawe,* ed. H. C. Fanshawe (London, John Lane, 1907), p. 84; *Two East Anglian Diaries 1641–1729: Isaac Archer and William Coe,* ed. M. Storey (Suffolk Records Society, 36, 1994), p. 160; *The Diary of Ralph Josselin, 1616–83,* ed. A. Macfarlane (British Academy Records of Social and Economic History, new series, 3, 1976), pp. 201–3.

28   R. A. Houlbrooke (ed.), *English Family Life, 1576–1716: An*

Anthology from Diaries (Oxford, Blackwell, 1988), pp. 142–4; *Diary of Ralph Josselin*, pp. 114–15; *Two East Anglian Diaries*, pp. 160–1, 166–7.

29   *Diary of Josselin*, p. 335; *Autobiography of Thornton*, pp. 126–7, 262–3; *The Life of Adam Martindale, written by himself*, ed. R. Parkinson (Chetham Society, old series, 4, 1845), p. 109.

30   Janeway, *Token*, I, preface containing directions to children (unpaginated).

31   F. L. Cross (ed.), *The Oxford Dictionary of the Christian Church* (3rd edn, ed. E. A. Livingstone, Oxford, Oxford University Press, 1997), p. 151.

32   Vincent, *The Saints Triumph*, p. 33.

33   S. Fleming, *Children and Puritanism: The Place of Children in the Life and Thought of the New England Churches 1620–1847* (New Haven and London, Yale University Press, 1933), pp. 1, 87, 90–1, 153, 178, 182. This old but thorough study draws on English works such as Janeway's and White's, both of which were reprinted several times in America, and describes patterns of behaviour very similar to those which appear in Janeway's *Token*.

34   G. R. Taylor, *The Angel Makers: A Study in the Psychological Origins of Historical Change, 1750–1850* (London, Heinemann, 1958), p. 313.

35   Sommerville, *Discovery of Childhood*, p. 31. The most sympathetic and perceptive treatment of Janeway's work is perhaps Gillian Avery's, in 'The Puritans and Their Heirs', pp. 109–12. She describes it as 'one of the most powerful pieces of writing ever produced for children', and mentions its 'tenderness' and 'sweet artless simplicity'. (Nathanael Vincent, describing Janeway's character in his funeral sermon, first mentioned the sweetness of his natural temper and disposition: *The Saints Triumph*, p. 32.)

Silent witnesses? Children and the breakdown of domestic and social order in early modern England

It was the privilege of children, according to the influential Phillipe Ariès, that during the early modern period they were rarely witnesses to the conflicts and problems of adult life. Childhood in this period, he argues, was marked as a separate stage of life by subjecting children 'to a special treatment, a sort of quarantine' in which they were isolated and 'safeguarded' from the adult world.[1] This chapter will suggest that for most families achieving this 'quarantine' was a practical impossibility, and that children were frequently present during familial and community discord. But while witnessing disputes may have played a crucial role in the formative experiences of many children, contemporaries were uneasy about children repeating in the courtroom what they had seen or heard of the adult world. As a result children as bystander witnesses were rarely called to testify. It will be shown that adult reluctance to allow children to speak about what they had witnessed reveals the limitations of understandings of childhood in pre-Lockean society. For the concept of child development was one that was confined to the physical, and there was an inability or unwillingness to accept that witnessing the breakdown of domestic or social order during childhood could affect an individual's subsequent psychological or emotional make-up.[2] As we shall see, evidence from legal records, diaries and autobiographies suggests that few adults in early modern England recognised that they held responsibility for the mental as well as the physical and spiritual well-being of their children.

The role of children in domestic and community quarrels can

tell us much of adult attitudes towards them. The apparently harmless activities of children could provoke a torrent of abuse. When Frances Gough's son was sent to buy a farthing's worth of apples from his neighbour Joan Wyatt in spring 1666, he was promptly sent home with the message for his mother that she 'kept none but thieves in her house'. Frances went straight across to Joan's house to discover what she meant by telling her son such things, only to be called a 'whore, Brazen faced whore and Brazen faced Jade'.[3] Although, as one witness stated, 'the occasion of the said difference was about their children', one suspects that this incident was the culmination of a longer-term disagreement between the two women. In many cases, it appears probable that children were easy targets for abuse which was intended primarily for their mothers. At a time when modern scientific testing was unknown, paternity could be a matter of opinion, and the visual appearance of children was thought to speak volumes about their parentage. 'Thou ... is John Hedley's bastard ... see thou art as like John Hedley as if he had spit thee out of his mouth', cried Mary Bryan to the daughter of Anne Hudspeth in Pilgrim Street, Newcastle, in 1629.[4] As Ann Holliday stood holding her child in Love Lane in Stepney in 1671 Margaret Cowper pointed to it and said 'that child ... is a bastard and like a man in Wapping and you are a whore'.[5] Attacks on children whose mothers were thought unchaste could become more violent. Robert Heaton rushed to the assistance of 'the child of Matthew Rutter's' who was being beaten by the mill at Cramlington, Northumbria, for fear that Ann Ellergill 'should do the child some harm for that she was in a great fury and rage'. 'Whore's bird go home and tell thy mother that Michael Lawson gave her six pounds in gold for occupying her', Ann said once she was forced to release the child.[6] One witness related how whenever Elizabeth Browne's children were seen by Sarah Overy in the streets of Stepney she called them 'whore's bastards'.[7] Mary West went home crying in 1664 when Margaret Siseman boasted that at least 'my mother never came to London to look for a father for her child when she was with child'.[8] Walter Lewis was in an alehouse insulting and striking John Bath before Christmas 1663. When John Bath's wife, Anne, entered with her child, who began to cry at the scene, Walter demanded to know 'whose child is this', and declared of Anne Bath, 'she is a whore I warrant her, her husband never got this

child', and her husband 'was not able to get thee children'.[9]
Adults in these cases used children to play upon the fears of their
parents. By questioning their legitimacy neighbours could place
doubt over a mother's chastity and a father's potency, both before
and after wedlock.

As children often shared the same domestic spaces as their
parents it seems highly probable that they were among the first to
know when relationships between their parents were breaking
down. When a neighbour came to investigate rumours that Isabell
Rawdon in Burdon, county Durham had been playing the whore
with Christopher Dickon whilst her husband was away around
Christmas 1636, he went straight to her children and asked them
'if . . . Christopher Dickon was not then in the same house', one
of them answering that 'he was then in the Chamber'. The continual presence of children with their mothers could make such illicit
unions difficult. Richard Arckley, another neighbour to the
Rawdon household, 'having a child sick' one night, rose out of
bed to see Christopher Dickon talking to Isabell Rawdon under
her chamber window. According to Richard, Christopher asked
Isabell 'where the maid was', and 'where her little boys were', to
which she replied 'that her Maid was in the loft and one of the
boys was in bed with her'. When Isabell let Christopher into her
house, curiosity got the better of the neighbour Richard, and he
went to stand under the Rawdons' window. He heard
Christopher try to persuade Isabell to go to bed with him, but she
at first denied him, saying that 'she durst not do because the boy
was in her bed'.[10] The practice of children or young people
sharing beds with their elders could be in other cases more fortu-
itous for the adults involved. When Jane Rand, a widow of
Gateside, county Durham was accused of being a whore one night
in 1622, she was able to produce Elizabeth Smith, described as 'a
young woman and neighbour's child', to testify that she was the
one who had been sharing Jane's bed on the night in question.[11]

For some young people, the discovery that their words could be
crucial in alleviating or confirming suspicions concerning adult
sexual reputation was no doubt exhilarating, and let them experience a degree of power usually denied to their age group. But for
others, the occasion could prove overwhelming and frightening.
When Catherine Jemmat of Plymouth came to write her memoirs
in 1762 and recalled her childhood, she wrote of an occasion

when her father, Admiral Yeo, had learnt from 'some busy
meddler' that his second wife, whom he had married when she
was nineteen, and Catherine just five years old, had been unfaithful in his absence. Admiral Yeo hurried home and, assuming that
his daughter would know whether her stepmother had been
unfaithful, 'sent post-haste to examine me, whether any gentleman came to the house when he was absent? I shuddered at the
question; and answered, that there never had been any; that I
believed slander itself could impeach her of no crime, except that
being too reserved might be construed into one.' After many
years, Catherine Jemmat could still recall the emotional impact of
her father's words; 'I shuddered at the question'. That her father
had questioned his five-year-old child, rather than his wife, and
had placed so much weight on her words, believing that it was
from her that he would learn the truth, is revealing. As a child
Catherine clearly lived in fear of her father, a 'single nod' of
disapproval from him, she notes, 'struck terror into the whole
family'. Her father knew that she would not dare to lie to him, yet
as a young girl Catherine had already learnt the importance of
chastity to a married woman, and hence recognised the gravity of
her answer.[12]

Children could also become enmeshed in violent struggles
between their parents. Elizabeth and John Harbin of Yeovil,
Somerset had been married about four years in 1669 when
Elizabeth brought a cruelty suit against her husband. Ann Lacey,
a servant in the Harbin household noted that on one occasion
when John tried to beat his wife, one of his sons wrenched from
him a kitchen pot which he was threatening to throw, whilst
another son pitifully cried out, 'Oh Lord you will kill my
mother'.[13] Although it was very unusual, a husband's violence
could extend to his children. In many ways Sir Oliver Boteler was
an exceptionally violent man who subjected his family to over
sixteen years of violence before his wife, Lady Ann, sued him for
cruelty in 1672.[14] He was obsessive about maintaining his control
over his household. Sir Oliver viewed his children as threatening
to his position of power in several ways. First, he could not be
certain that they were legitimate. Were they instead the offspring
of an intruder to his marital bed? Secondly, his jealousy of his
wife extended to the affection which his children held for their
mother. Such affection, in Sir Oliver's eyes, could serve to lessen

his authority. To reassert his position, and undermine that of his wife, he attempted to force his children to revile their mother. He told his three-year-old son that if he heard him say again that he loved his mother, he would whip him, and commanded his eight-year-old daughter Elizabeth to strike her mother, who was then pregnant, on the belly and give her 'a box on the ear', otherwise he said he would 'never endure her'. Sir Oliver was so angry that his son 'ran to his mother' after he had whipped him on an earlier occasion, that he 'snatched him up again, and whipped him again ... [causing] the said child and his said Mother to cry out very grievously'. His wife loved their children 'so dearly' that he knew 'no other way ... to break her heart' than to kill them, he was overheard saying. Hence one morning when the eight-year-old Elizabeth came into Sir Oliver's room, 'kneeled down' and asked her father for his blessing, he 'took her up and whipped her very cruelly'. When he took his daughter out of the room, Lady Ann fell on her knees and begged him not to beat the child anymore. At which he 'in great fury said if anybody came near to save her he would throw her ... downstairs and break her neck, and therewith all held her over the rails of the stairs two stairs high'. Dangling the child over the stairway, with his wife and servants crying and begging him not to drop her, Sir Oliver dramatically demonstrated his power in the household. In contrast, Lady Ann's relative powerlessness to prevent the violence of her husband was summarised by one witness, who described Ann as 'a child carrying herself continually with wonderful meekness and patience'.[15]

The scale of terror which Sir Oliver brought on his household was unusual, but some aspects of his behaviour were found in other families. Theobold Townson of Melcombe Regis, Dorset, was described by one witness in 1699 as 'holding his wife's hands and telling his son John (a Child about five or six years old) who had then an oaken stick in his hand to strike or beat ... his mother and cried out ... Jack knock the bitch on the head'.[16] By making children attack their mothers, these fathers were forcing children to make an intolerable choice of loyalties between their parents. William Fleetwood and James Nelson, influential eighteenth-century writers on childrearing, both lamented how children could be used by one parent against the other in their disputes.[17] Children, it seems, could be as much the victims of marital breakdown as their parents.

Of course, children were not just witnesses to the marital troubles of their parents. At a young age, many children commenced domestic service or apprenticeship, and lived in the households where they worked. Historians have noted the importance of servants and apprentices as witnesses in marriage separation suits. Servants could also become the focus of their master's or mistresses adulterous intentions.[18] Simon Forman's autobiography, which was written in the second half of the sixteenth century, provides us with one account of what these young people could witness. Simon entered an apprenticeship with a hosier when he was about fourteen years old. He could not agree with his mistress, but he found to his relief, that neither could his master. His master and mistress, he noted:

> often times ... were also at square, in so much that twice he [his master] had like to have killed her by casting a pair of tailor's shears at her, for once they went so near her, that as she was going in at a door, he nailed her clothes and smock at her buttocks to the door, and the points of the shears went clean through the door, and she hung fast by the tail; whereupon he swore in his wrath that if ever he died before her, he would never give her anything.

Simon became a confidant and trusted male companion for his master. 'Many times when Simon and his master went to his farm together, some two miles off in the country, they would one complain to another of his mistress and her pride', he recalled. In the face of a 'headstrong, and proud fantastical woman', as Simon described her, the differences of age and status between these two men fell away. According to Simon's version of events, their shared gender and subjection to a 'headstrong' woman bound them together.[19]

It is clear from a range of sources that in the course of everyday life, while playing, working, or even trying to sleep, children could encounter domestic and community discord. Adults, such as the seventeenth-century Puritan minister, Adam Martindale, were often impressed that even very young children could remember the details of what they had witnessed. When his three-year-old daughter and her young companions testified to the rape of another child by a local fisherman, he noted in his autobiography that 'the great wonder was this: though it was many months between the commitment and arraignment of this man, and my child was so young as aforesaid, and though they were oft examined before magistrates, ministers, jurors, and judges, they told the same tale punctually, without ever contradicting themselves or one another, and answered cross questions wonderfully.'[20] The contemporary proverb, 'the child says nothing but what it heard by the fire', reflected the popular view that children were prone to repeat adult conversation they had overheard within the home.[21]

By witnessing the quarrels of their parents, masters, and neighbours, children soon learnt how as adults they would be expected to fulfil various roles in their families and communities according to their social status and gender. It was failure to pursue these roles which could lead to conflict. Having learnt these lessons, there were occasions when children could be more than witnesses, and also play a part in enforcing moral codes. Hence Lucy Sutton told Ellinor Thurben that when Ellinor was discovered by children illicitly having sex with one John Aynsley in the White Tower of Newcastle 'boys and children chased her from thence with stones'.[22] There is little doubt that many children had an early initiation into the world of male and female reputation or honour. As they grew older, learning to defend the reputation of oneself and one's mother could play an important part in a child's transition to adulthood. Ann Holt, and Elizabeth Ashley who was aged about sixteen years, both took their mother's parts in a quarrel over cockfighting in 1664. When Elizabeth said to Ann 'my mother never had a bastard by a Grocer', Ann angrily replied 'you brazon faced impudent whore'. Both had resorted to sexual insult.[23] The dispute between the Flood and Addis households was also triggered by two cocks fighting. When the fifteen-year-old Martha Flood, who lived with her parents, told her neighbour John Addis that her father did not want their cock to fight with the Addis's cock, she was met with a violent response. John Addis called her 'bastardly Young Jade, and bad her to be gone out of his yard, saying that if she would not go out he would kick her out', 'hubbing and thulling' her 'against a neighbour's door'. Further insults followed between Martha Flood's mother and John Addis's wife. In the defamation suit initiated by her mother which resulted, Martha Flood acted as a witness in court, telling her story to support her mother's case.[24] This defence of a mother's sexual reputation was not restricted to daughters. The apprentice son of Elizabeth Hawlings acted as a witness in court for his mother after he had heard her slandered as a whore in Hornsey in 1665, and sixteen-year-old James Taylor spoke in addition to his elder brother when their mother was accused of playing the whore and being infected with the pox in 1676.[25] Of course, these children's inheritance may have been at stake if their mother had been engaging in illicit sex. But their presence in the courtroom may have been motivated by more than just self-interest. Their willingness to testify could also be interpreted as a sign that these older children had become integral members of their families able to accept responsibilities, rather than be shielded from them. Demonstrating a loyalty to family ties, these young people could do more than simply witness adult quarrels, they could also help to resolve them.

But whereas young people did sometimes testify in the church courts during defamation suits, they were very rarely heard as witnesses during the marriage separation suits of their parents. Of ninety-two separation cases that reached the personal answer and/or witness deposition stage in the proceedings of the court of Arches between 1660 and 1700, for example, there were only four cases in which children acted as witnesses. In all four of these cases, the marriages which had broken down were remarriages, and the children who spoke were stepchildren to one of the parties.[26] We know from adult depositions that couples had children in at least twenty-eight other cases. Indeed, the presence or behaviour of children could trigger their parents' quarrels. For example, Rachael Norcott's sister recalled in 1666 how Rachael was once thrown to the ground by her husband when Rachael tried to stop him from violently disciplining their son.[27] In many cases children of the parties were obviously too young to testify, as marital disputes centred upon the legitimacy of a new-born baby. The relative absence of older children as witnesses may have rested with the law. Certainly, according to Romano-canonical theory, no child under the age of fourteen was permitted to act as a witness in the church courts, and no child could testify on behalf of a parent. Some legal theorists such as Henry Conset in his 1685 handbook on the church courts only gave consideration to the issue of minors as plaintiffs, not as witnesses. Richard Burn, on the other hand, declared in his influential guide of 1763 that no close kin, domestics, or other dependants should act as witnesses in the church courts. But clearly, the occasional appearance of child witnesses in some types of suits in the church courts, a practice which continued into the nineteenth century, and the frequent depositions taken from other kin, servants, and women, who were other categories of witnesses originally barred from giving evidence, shows that practice could deviate from theory.[28]

The words of children could be taken very seriously in early modern England. Work on children who prophesied God's word, or who were possessed by witchcraft has shown that children's words could be accorded a privileged status.[29] But such occasions were rare, and to be certain of an audience these children frequently accompanied their words with extreme or dramatic behaviour: throwing fits, writhing, or screaming. The adults connected with these children often tried to control or manipulate their words. To provide a formal platform such as the courtroom for children to speak was to allow children the opportunity to challenge adult authority. In the church courts, where witness statements were not taken in open court, but were recorded and submitted as written documents, parties still appear to have had a preference for choosing, when possible, adult bystander witnesses over child ones. The fear that children did not have the discretion or developed reason to deploy what they had witnessed in a responsible way which would protect adult interests was reflected in popular proverbs, and could be used to discredit them if they did provide testimony for the courts. 'What children hear at home soon flies abroad' ran one proverb; 'children pick up words as pigeons peas and utter them again as God shall please', warned another.[30] Children were asked whether they understood the nature of an oath, and their statements were questioned if it could be shown that they had been subject to adult influence or intimidation. Adult witnesses who spoke in defence of William Wood in a defamation case of 1668, for example, tried to discredit the words of the witness John Budder, who was estimated to be between the age of twelve and fourteen years, because he was 'but a little boy', who was bound to speak in defence of his master, 'a hasty chollerick man', of whom all the servants lived 'in very great awe'.[31]

It seems highly likely, then, that the letter of the law was employed selectively to exclude children from acting as bystander witnesses. For young children to comment on the disciplinary business of the church courts, which so often dealt with deviant language or behaviour of a sexual nature may have seemed particularly inappropriate. It was unthinkable that children should testify against their natural parents, even though they could also be victims of marital violence. For children's primary duty was to remain silent, and according to the biblical injunction, honour their parents. If children were witnesses to their parents' faults, according to William Gouge, children should 'cover their parents' infirmities' by 'passing by them . . . and taking no notice of them, and also by concealing them from others as much as they can'.[32]

   The duty of children to be silent and avoid speaking critically of their elders appears to have been followed even when children themselves reached adulthood. In diaries and autobiographies from the seventeenth and eighteenth centuries criticisms about upbringing, or comments on the quality of relationships between parents are extremely rare. When any statements were given they were usually in an apologetic fashion. Francis Place described in his autobiography the severe beatings he received as a child from his father, but then added that his father intended such punishment for the 'good' of his children, and that such forms of discipline were common in past times.[33] Remarks on the nature of spousal relationships appear confined to those made by stepchildren about relationships between a natural parent and a step-parent. These children appear to have been acutely aware of their potential to disrupt the marriage partnership. Ralph Josselin, for example, was not fond of his father's second wife whom he married when Ralph was about fourteen years old. But he later wrote that, 'I remember not that I ever caused any debate or division betwixt them for anything'.[34] Other stepchildren did attempt to cause trouble in a parent's remarriage, showing that children could be more than simply pawns in the disputes around them. Charles Varley, a farmer's son in the early eighteenth century, was not prepared to tolerate the treatment he received from his stepmother and by telling his father caused quarrels between his parents. He later criticised his stepmother for her cruelty in his autobiography, and claimed that at the age of fourteen he ran away into service to escape her ill-usage.[35] Once in service, the indenture or agreement of service made between an apprentice and master gave masters a formal obligation to provide apprentices with training in morals and manners as well as a craft or trade.[36] But apprentices very rarely attempted to break with their service on the grounds that their masters were not providing a stable or moral environment in which to live. The London apprentice who told his master 'that he would not tarry with him for he kept a whore in his house' was probably highly unusual.[37]

In the seventeenth century, many contemporaries recognised that children were prone to imitating the adult world around them. Early modern conduct-book writers saw children as impressionable, and as a result, many, including Gouge, the anonymous writer of *The Office of Christian Parents*, John Dod and Robert Cleaver, instructed parents to be guarded in their speech when they were in front of their children. Parents 'must be careful that they do not speak or tell any foolish tales, bawdy rhymes or ungodly speeches before their children, lest they infect their tender wits with folly and astonishment', Dod and Cleaver wrote.[38] Indeed, this was a period in which the influence of adults was thought so great that their curses upon children were believed to have the power to physically deform babies as they lay in the womb.[39] But the impression or impact of the adult world upon children was conceived only in physical terms. The authorities of early modern England were occasionally prepared to punish adults who had subjected the children in their care to extreme physical cruelty or abuse.[40] However, there are few indications that adults at this time understood that there was any possibility of psychological damage to a child who witnessed severe or violent incidents of conflict. It is very difficult to find instances of adults who tried to shield their children from what we might see today as potentially negative childhood experiences. How do we interpret Hester Watson's words to Ely Quarter Sessions in March 1743, for example, that she was beaten by her husband, 'after he had first ordered his son John Watson junior to go out of the House and to shut ... the Door'? Given the limitations of early modern understandings of children it seems probable that Hester's husband acted in this way for self-protection, believing that his son could have acted to prevent the beating or later speak to the Justice of the Peace against him, or even out of a sense of shame for his violence, rather than because he wished to protect his child from witnessing a harrowing scene.[41] The presence of many children during the disputes of the adults around them may suggest that they did not often act to inhibit the behaviour of adults. Of course, witnessing disputes may not always have been a negative experience for children, and may sometimes have helped them to learn important lessons in conflict negotiation and resolution.[42] Later events in childhood or adolescence may also have proved to be influential in shaping personality or psychological development.[43] But the power of adult insults on children once they were born was rarely acknowledged; there was only one defamation case heard in the Restoration court of Arches which took the child's reputation into account when it calculated the damage that the slander of bastard had incurred.[44] Yet the insult may have raised a child's doubts and fears over the identity of their father, and the memory of the insult could remain with them for the rest of their lives. The Lancashire apprentice Roger Lowe, for instance, had to fight to keep his loved one in the 1660s after she had heard a false rumour that he was illegitimate, and was ready to break off their relationship on this basis.[45] The church courts seldom gave thought to the welfare of children as they considered whether to grant a couple separation from bed and board when marriage relationships broke down irreparably. This was even though evidence of cruelty to children appears to have been used by some women to substantiate their claims for separation. Witnesses for Mary Whiston, for example, chose to tell the court of Arches of her husband's flagrant disregard for the impact of his behaviour on his children. They reported how on one occasion when James Whiston was going to beat her in February 1669, and Mary begged him not to because it would make her child cry, he angrily replied, 'you whore let it cry'.[46] Children could subsequently be left in the care of these violent men, since in this period, even if a wife was successful in her separation suit, she lost all legal rights for access to her children.[47]

'The most striking feature' about the ages of patients who visited the physician Richard Napier in the seventeenth century was that there were so few children. From this Michael MacDonald concludes that 'seventeenth-century parents were less ready than we are to think that their children were psychologically disturbed'.[48] It is the contention of this chapter that before John Locke's ideas of individual child development took hold, and children began to be regarded as beings with vulnerable and sensitive emotional lives of their own, adults did not share a concept of the psychologically damaged child, nor did they have a common understanding of how psychological damage in childhood could be caused. For these concepts to develop the definition of child health would have to be extended to include mental as well as physical well being, and crucially, would require adults to accept wider terms of responsibility for the welfare of their children. Until that responsibility was acknowledged, children could be very effectively silenced in early modern England.

Notes

I would like to thank Anthony Fletcher for his helpful comments on this chapter. An earlier version was also given to the Cambridge Early Modern Seminar, and I am grateful to all who attended for their constructive criticisms.

1 P. Ariès, *Centuries of Childhood: A Social History of Family Life* (New York, Vintage, 1962), pp. 128, 133, 411–13.
2 For the most helpful work by modern-day psychologists on this issue see J. H. Grych and F. D. Fincham, 'Marital Conflict and Children's Adjustment: A Cognitive-Contextual Framework', *Psychological Bulletin*, 108 (1990), 267–90; I am grateful to F. D. Fincham for sending me a copy of this article. For a historical attempt to relate the experiences of childhood to later adult development in seventeenth-century New England see J. Demos, 'Developmental Perspectives on the History of Childhood', in T. K. Rabb and R. I. Rotberg (eds), *The Family in History: Interdisciplinary Essays* (London, Harper and Row, 1971). For the best summary of the impact of John Locke's work on attitudes to children see H. Cunningham, *Children and Childhood in Western Society since 1500* (Harlow, Longman, 1995), pp. 62–5.
3 Lambeth Palace Library, London, Court of Arches (hereafter CA), Case 3843 (case numbers taken from J. Houston, *Index of the Cases in the Records of the Court of Arches in Lambeth Palace Library, 1660–1913* [1972]) (1666), Deposition (hereafter Eee) 2, f. 229v–230r; for other similar examples see L. Gowing, *Domestic Dangers: Women, Words, and Sex in Early Modern London* (Oxford, Oxford University Press, 1996), pp. 116–77.
4 Durham University Library, Durham Diocese Consistory Court

Deposition Book (hereafter DDR.V.), 12. f. 177r.

5   CA, Case 4695 (1671), Eee4, f. 393r.

6   DDR.V.11, ff. 518v–519r.

7   CA, Case 1360 (1666), Eee2, f. 169v.

8   CA, Case 9813 (1664), Eee1, f. 713r.

9   CA, Case 598 (1664), Eee1, ff. 68v–70r.

10 DDR, Box 1636–7, *Rawdon* v. *Dickon.*

11 DDR.V. 11, f. 185v.

12 *The Memoirs of Mrs Catherine Jemmat,* 2nd ed. (London, 1771), pp. 5, 10–12.

13 CA, Case 4163 (1669), Eee4, ff. 81–82v.

14 Hence I cannot agree with L. Stone who believes that there is 'nothing uncommon about the cruelty' in this case in his *Broken Lives* (Oxford, Oxford University Press, 1993), p. 37.

15 CA, Case 1041 (1672), Eee4, ff. 816v–818r, 852r–869r; for further assessment of this case see E. Foyster, 'Male Honour, Social Control and Wife Beating in Late Stuart England', *Transactions of the Royal Historical Society,* 6th series, 6 (1996), 215–24.

16 CA, Case 9240 (1699), Eee8, f. 635v.

17 W. Fleetwood, *The Relative Duties of Parents and Children* (London, 1705), pp. 13–14; J. Nelson, *An Essay on the Government of Children* (London, 1756), p. 172.

18 P. M. Humfrey, '"I saw through a large chink in the partition . . ." What the Servants Knew', in V. Frith (ed.), *Women and History: Voices of Early Modern England* (Toronto, Coach House Press, 1995); J. Lane, *Apprenticeship in England, 1600–1914* (London, UCL Press, 1996), pp. 216, 223.

19 J. O. Halliwell (ed.), *The Autobiography and Personal Diary of Dr Simon Forman* (London, 1849), p. 10.

20 R. Parkinson, (ed.), *The Life of Adam Martindale,* Chetham Society (Manchester, 1845), p. 207.

21 M. P. Tilley, *A Dictionary of Proverbs in England in the Sixteenth and Seventeenth Centuries* (Ann Arbor, Mich., University of Michigan Press, 1950), C300.

22 DDR.V.12, ff. 47v.

23 The argument resulted in two cases, one brought by Elizabeth Ashley, and one by the mother of Ann Holt, Margery King; CA, Case 250 (1664), Eee1, ff. 612–13, and CA, Case 5348 (1664), Eee1, ff. 669v–673r.

24 CA, Case 3379 (1667), Eee2, ff. 549–553r, 631v–633v.

25 CA, Case 940 (1665), Eee2, f. 2v–3r; CA, Case 8986 (1676), Eee6, f. 44v–48r.

26 I discuss the issue of children who acted as witnesses in the case of the breakdown of remarriages in 'Marrying the Experienced Widow in Early Modern England: The Male Perspective', in S. Cavallo and L. Warner (eds), *Widowhood in Medieval and Early Modern Europe* (Harlow, Longman, forthcoming).

27 CA, Case 6659 (1666), Eee2, f. 102r.

28 H. Conset, *The Practice of the Spiritual or Ecclesiastical Courts* (London, 1685), p. 51; R. Burn, *Ecclesiastical Law*, 3rd edn (London, 1775), vol. II, p. 208; C. Donahue, 'Proof by Witnesses in the Church Courts of Medieval England: An Imperfect Reception of the Learned Law', in M. S. Arnold, T. A. Green, S. A. Scully and S. D. White (eds), *On the Laws and Customs of England* (Chapel Hill, University of North Carolina Press, 1981); B. J. Shapiro, *'Beyond Reasonable Doubt' and 'Probable Cause': Historical Perspectives on the Anglo-American Law of Evidence* (Berkeley, University of California Press, 1991), p. 189; for children as occasional witnesses in the church courts of the nineteenth century see P. Morris, 'Defamation and Sexual Reputation in Somerset, 1733–1850' (unpublished Ph.D. thesis, University of Warwick, 1985), pp. 356–64; for the status of child bystander witnesses in the secular courts see C. B. Herrup, *The Common Peace: Participation and the Criminal Law in Seventeenth-Century England* (Cambridge, Cambridge University Press, 1989), p. 83; J. R. Spencer and R. Flin, *The Evidence of Children: The Law and the Psychology* (London, Blackstone, 1990).

29 A. Walsham, '"Out of the mouths of babes and sucklings": Prophecy, Puritanism, and Childhood in Elizabethan Suffolk', and S. Hardman Moore, '"Such perfecting of praise out of the mouth of a babe": Sarah Wight as Child Prophet', in D. Wood (ed.), *The Church and Childhood*, Studies in Church History, 31 (Oxford, Oxford University Press, 1994), pp. 285–99 and 313–24 respectively; and J. A. Sharpe, 'Disruption in the Well-Ordered Household: Age, Authority, and Possessed Young People', in P. Griffiths, A. Fox and S. Hindle (eds), *The Experience of Authority in Early Modern England* (London, Macmillan, 1996), pp. 187–212.

30 Tilley, *A Dictionary of Proverbs*, C344, C333.

31 CA, Case 10152 (1668), Eee3, ff. 766r, 768r, 772v, 824v; John

Budder's statement is contained within CA, Case 10232, (1669), Eee3, ff. 453v–454r; for young people being questioned about their understanding of oaths see Gowing, *Domestic Dangers*, pp. 50–1.

32   W. Gouge, *Of Domesticall Duties* (London, 1622), pp. 471–2; for more on children's duty to remain silent see J. Kamensky, 'Talk like a Man: Speech, Power, and Masculinity in Early New England', *Gender and History*, 8:1 (1996), 28–30.

33   M. Thrale (ed.), *The Autobiography of Francis Place (1771–1854)* (Cambridge, Cambridge University Press, 1972), pp. 61–2; I am grateful to Angela Thomas for bringing my attention to this autobiography.

34   *The Diary of the Reverend Ralph Josselin 1616–1683* Camden Society, 3rd series, vol. XV (1908), p. 3.

35   C. Varley, *The Modern Farmers Guide* (Glasgow, 1768), vol. I, pp. v–xi; for more on the quality of stepfamily relationships see, S. Collins, 'British Stepfamily Relationships, 1500–1800', *Journal of Family History*, 16:4 (1991), 331–44.

36   Lane, *Apprenticeship*, pp. 74–5, 214.

37   As cited in P. Griffiths, *Youth and Authority: Formative Experiences in England 1560–1640* (Oxford, Oxford University Press, 1996), p. 242.

38   Gouge, *Of Domesticall Duties*, p. 543; Anon., *The Office of Christian Parents* (Cambridge, 1616), p. 57; J. Dod and R. Cleaver, *A Godly Form of Householde Government* (London, 1630), Q4.

39   I am grateful to Tim Stretton for drawing my attention to this; for an example see DDR.V.10B, ff. 298–9.

40   Lane, *Apprenticeship*, ch. 10; M. Pelling, 'Child health as a social value in early modern England', *Social History of Medicine*, 1:2 (1988), 135–64.

41   Cambridge University Library, Ely Quarter Sessions Files, 48 (bound in Roll for April 1748).

42   A good example of this is provided by Hermann von Weinsberg's memories of his childhood in sixteenth-century Cologne, in which he commented on how his parents overcame their differences; see S. Ozment, *When Fathers Ruled: Family Life in Reformation Europe* (Cambridge, Mass., Harvard University Press, 1983), p. 55.

43   This point is made in L. A. Pollock, *Forgotten Children: Parent–Child Relations from 1500 to 1900* (Cambridge, Cambridge University Press, 1983), pp. 27–8.

44   CA, Case 3367 (1668), Eee3, ff. 91–92.

45 R. Adair, *Courtship, Illegitimacy and Marriage in Early Modern England* (Manchester, Manchester University Press, 1996), p. 89.
46 CA, Case 9870 (1669), Eee3, f. 555v.
47 L. Stone, *Road to Divorce: England 1530–1987* (Oxford, Oxford University Press, 1990), pp. 4–5, 13; R. Phillips, *Untying the Knot: A Short History of Divorce* (Cambridge, Cambridge University Press, 1991), pp. 233–4; Peter Earle also comments on the rarity of comments concerning children in the depositions of marriage separation suits, and the lack of provision for their welfare in *The Making of the English Middle Class: Business, Society and Family Life in London 1660–1730* (London, Methuen, 1989), p. 234.
48 M. MacDonald, *Mystical Bedlam: Madness, Anxiety, and Healing in Seventeenth-Century England* (Cambridge, Cambridge University Press, 1983), pp. 42–3.

'A denial of innocence': female juvenile victims of rape and the English legal system in the eighteenth century

In the 1796 trial of David Scott for the rape of Mary Homewood, Mr Knapp, council for the prosecution, made the following statement to the court:

> The case will depend upon the credit you shall think yourselves bound to give to the story of the prosecutrix. Observe, she is of the tender age of eleven; we shall be inclined, perhaps, to hope that from those tender years her heart had not received any taint or corruption; yet, we know, in this great metropolis, young as that person may be, it may pass into the hearts of persons, so young, to forget that duty they owe to society, and sometimes to have a very wicked intent at so tender an age.[1]

Mary Homewood underwent an ordeal on the witness stand in which the defence lawyer questioned the truthfulness of her claims. He interrogated her regarding every circumstance surrounding the alleged assault and went on to challenge the girl's claims of a good character and innocent nature, as well as suggesting that her parents had persuaded her to tell such a story for financial purposes. David Scott was eventually found guilty of rape on the strength of medical testimony which proved that penetration had occurred and that violence had been used to achieve it. He was sentenced to death.

Mary was one of sixteen girls below the age of fourteen who pursued allegations of rape through the Old Bailey in the period 1734–97. Each one faced disbelief and censure in a middle-class courtroom in which the honesty of any female who claimed to have been sexually assaulted was questioned. The many obstacles women faced in trying to secure a successful prosecution against their assailants in the eighteenth century have led historians to recognise that many incidents of rape failed to reach the trial stage.[2] This chapter discusses prosecutions against child rape that did reach the courtroom. It considers how the difficulties faced by legal officials in examining claims of rape were further complicated when the prosecutrix was below the age of twelve.

Historians of sexual crime have tended not to focus their research on reported incidences of child rape. Instead, their work has concentrated upon adult victims of rape with little distinction drawn between treatment received by different age groups in the courtroom. Studies by Anna Clark and Antony Simpson do highlight the high number of rape cases in the eighteenth century involving juvenile victims, yet there is a tendency to categorise these along with adult female victims.[3] It is important to recognise that these young victims faced a different set of obstacles on the witness stand to their adult counterparts. The responses to the stories told by these girls were influenced by ideas about vulnerability and innocence which society held in connection with young females. Changing perceptions of childhood in eighteenth-century England, as highlighted originally by Ariès and explored by writers such as Shorter and Stone, left the child rape victim in a predicament where sexually she had become an adult but socially remained a child.[4]

The words of Mary Homewood's lawyer show that the veracity of a story told by an eleven-year-old girl on the witness stand could easily be brought into question.[5] Fears that the immoral values of the 'great metropolis' could corrupt impressionable young minds made juries suspicious that rape claims were made for financial gain or to cover up a sexual indiscretion. Mr Knapp made the courtroom aware that even at the young age of eleven a girl could be open to such an evil as blackmail or to immorality. He concludes his long opening statement by saying that the judgement must rest upon the credit given by the jury to the story of the prosecutrix and – should she falter – then the defendant must be found innocent. Clearly much responsibility was placed upon the strength of the victim's story, but, as will be shown, expectations of a girl's innocence of sexual matters restricted her ability to describe what had occurred. The increasing emphasis on the role of parent as protector meant that the court frowned upon the claims of a girl who was seen to have been left in a vulnerable situation with a male. It was possible for the blame for an assault to be placed on the girl or her parents rather than the assailant.

Child rape made up 20 to 25 per cent of all sexual crimes tried in the Old Bailey in the eighteenth century. Antony Simpson identifies over fifty such cases covering a 100-year period.[6] It is in the middle to later eighteenth century, however, that these cases are the most illuminating. The changing nature of the Old Bailey Sessions Papers in the eighteenth century from sensationalist literature to a quasi-legal source had a significant impact upon their format. After 1797, the level of detail given about 'sensitive' cases was reduced drastically for the sake of public decency and information about rape trials became limited to the names of the defendant and the prosecutrix, their ages and occupations, witnesses called and the verdict. Earlier Sessions Papers allow access to complete trial transcripts demonstrating the victim's ordeal on the witness stand and the attitudes of legal professionals towards the crime of rape.

Sixteen trials for child rape have been identified as taking place in the period 1735 to 1797 and it is these that this chapter examines in depth. *R* v. *Scott* was one of five where the defendant was found guilty and sentenced to death. Eleven of the trials led to an acquittal of the charge of rape, a statistic which reflects the burden of proof faced by a female prosecutrix.[7] Of these eleven acquittals four of the defendants were retried on the lesser charge of assault with intent to commit a rape, a common procedure adopted by eighteenth-century courts. The procedure of reducing the charge and its implications for charges pursued by children will be examined later. The ages of the girls claiming to have been raped ranged from four and a half to fourteen, although the majority were between nine and eleven. No pattern can be established with regards to the age of child victims and the likelihood of conviction. The treatment of females below the age of twelve will therefore be examined in relation to the credibility given to their stories and how the veracity of their claims was challenged on the witness stand.

This chapter highlights the importance of examining the legal treatment of child victims of sexual crime as distinct from adults.[8] The fact that the notion of 'youth' was not recognised by the legal system in the eighteenth century meant that a young complainant could not expect any allowances to be made for her age in terms of the types of evidence required to prove that a crime had been committed. However, the appearance of a child victim on the witness stand raised a different set of issues about character, evidence and language than did that of an adult female prosecutrix. The prosecutions discussed here show how social conditions had left the young girls who appeared at the Old Bailey vulnerable to sexual assault and the extent to which the legal system apportioned blame for this. They show too that legal discrepancies regarding age made the young rape victim's fight for justice a difficult one. Paternalism and the emphasis on children remaining innocent of adult matters also influenced the way in which a trial for sexual crime was conducted. Juries in the eighteenth century were very reluctant to convict a man of rape, and the problems faced by victims in gaining a conviction could differ as a result of whether the complainant was an adult or a child. Expectations from society about a child's innocence of sexual matters and its need for protection were incompatible with social conditions which left many young girls vulnerable and, more significantly, with a legal system that made very few allowances for age.

Mary Homewood, at the age of eleven, worked as a pot-girl in the public house owned by her father.[9] The alleged assault by David Scott took place when she was asked to deliver beer to him at the dyehouse where he worked. She was sent alone into a predominantly male environment, something she was often required to do. The stories of assault told by other young girls in the Old Bailey show that the circumstances of the attack on Mary Homewood were not unusual. Frequently girls would be left in vulnerable situations. Young girls working for parents or employers were forced to live and work in adult social spheres, such as alehouses, or else in isolated environments. Ten-year-old Mary Matthews was employed at an alehouse when she alleged that Charles Earle burst into the room where she was working and raped her.[10] Jane Bell had the job of selling milk on her own at the entrance to Hyde Park, where it was common for her to start work at 6 a.m. and not return until past 9 p.m.[11] She was assaulted by a man who followed her as she returned from the park one evening.

These girls all tell stories of being left alone with adult males, something which was usual with regard to their role as an employee. There are examples of girls serving drink and food to men in alehouses and also entering the bedchambers of lodgers.[12] The need for young children to enter employment and assist in adult-dominated spheres frequently left them in the company of men with no degree of parental protection. Even if parents were aware of the potential threats facing young girls, poorer families could do little to change a daughter's working environment. Nevertheless, it is apparent that parents were questioned by the judges in the Old Bailey about the frequency with which they left their daughters unattended in the company of men. Hugh Cunningham argues that increasingly in the eighteenth century the issue of parental protection became bound up in humanist theories about childhood. As childhood became identified as a distinct phase of life parents came to be held responsible for maintaining it. Pollock comments that 'mothers and fathers have always had the concept of childhood, whereas those in power had to learn not so much what a child is, but that its helplessness could be exploited by society'.[13] These ideas seem to be borne out in the testimonies given to the Old Bailey. The father of Ann Thacker, aged eleven, was openly chastised by the judge for his failure to protect his child after Thomas Davenport was convicted of raping her.[14] Robert Thacker missed much of the trial as he was appearing at the Quarter Sessions charged with being 'in liquor'. When he did appear the judge informed him that the girl had been left open to assault as she had been alone in the house with Davenport, a lodger, whilst her father and stepmother were at a nearby alehouse. Social conditions and ideas had placed the girls who appeared before the Old Bailey in situations where they were frequently left in what could be termed 'dangerous' environments yet they were rendered powerless to do anything about it. Mary Homewood claims that she was too afraid of being beaten by her parents to refuse to serve drinks to men in the dyehouse.[15] Changing perceptions of the role of the parent meant that increasingly parents were expected to protect the innocence of their children, yet in reality economic pressures meant that this was something they had little control over.

Attempts to explain the prevalence of child rape in the eighteenth century have pointed to a prominent medical myth that sexual intercourse with a virgin could cure a venereal disease. Antony Simpson suggests that medical theory contributed to a 'defloration mania'.[16] Mr Knapp stated to the court in the trial of David Scott:

> I shall prove to you, that that too common idea of persons, having a certain disorder upon them which they foolishly think they can get rid of, by having connection with a young person, or a person that never had connection with man before, they think, by that connection, they can cure themselves; that is the fact that I understand.[17]

Legal jurists cited the above misconception as the one deployed as a defence in a number of rape trials in the eighteenth century.[18] The supposedly beneficial effects of sexual intercourse with a young virgin served to increase the vulnerability of young girls in eighteenth-century society.

Historians have tended to discuss sexual crime in terms of the power relationships between men and women.[19] However, it should be recognised that 'power' becomes a less significant concept in relation to the rape of female children. The popular idea that intercourse with a virgin was a treatment for sexually transmitted disease cannot be explained in terms of male dominance but instead as the exploitation of a medical misconception. In court records involving girls below the age of twelve the issue of control over their behaviour and safety had been transferred to the parents. Justice Rooke reprimands Mary Homewood's mother, saying 'you see what you have brought upon the child by your passion; I hope it will be a warning to you' after the mother admitted to having beaten Mary before she had had the opportunity of explaining about the sexual assault that had taken place.[20] The cases of child rape brought before the Old Bailey in the eighteenth century are important in illustrating the relationships between daughters and their parents in eighteenth-century urban London, more so than for examining issues of gender relations upon which work on sexual crime usually concentrates.

In 1777 the Reverend B. Russen was tried for the rape of Ann Mayne and three other young girls placed in his care.[21] As the master of a charity school Russen was in a position of authority over young children and trust as regards their parents. Russen's case provides an excellent example of how children were placed in situations with adult males where it was natural for the rest of society not to question whether this would prove threatening. The mother of ten-year-old Ann was bringing up her children alone and sent them to Russen's school while she worked. She claims in her testimony that she witnessed that the child appeared to be walking strangely and immediately took her to a surgeon without examining Ann, or her linen, herself. The mother assumed that her daughter had contracted an illness and did not suspect what had in fact occurred. Ann Mayne's mother believed she was leaving her child in the care of a respectable member of the clergy so had no reason to fear how she would be treated. Sarah Mayne faced criticism from the court, not for leaving her child at the charity school, but for failing to recognise the signs that an assault had taken place. Sarah Mayne could not be judged by the court for leaving her child while she went out to work but it was perceived that she should have been more aware of her daughter's situation.

It can be seen from the records of the Old Bailey that, in trials for the rape of a child, the vulnerability of young girls to such assault was recognised but it was deemed the responsibility of her parents or guardians to protect her from the risk of abuse. For example, in the case of Jane Bell, the young girl who sold milk at the gates of Hyde Park each day, it was her employer who was deemed responsible for the girl's vulnerability.[22] In the majority of testimonies the victim states that she was in an environment where she was alone with an adult male as the result of direct orders from her parents or employers. Therefore, the victim in child rape cases was not held accountable for leaving herself open to the risk of assault, as was commonly the case in trials involving adult women. According to eighteenth-century legal attitudes the vulnerability of childhood was something defined and subject to protection by adults.

Rape first became a felony by law under the 1275 Statute of Westminster.[23] However, it was not until 1576 that an additional bill drew a distinction between adult and child victims.[24] Although legally the age of consent in the eighteenth century was twelve, the 1576 Act had made any sexual intercourse with a child below the age of ten a felony. If a girl was between the ages of ten and twelve then sexual intercourse only constituted a misdemeanour and non-consent had to be proved for the charge of rape. Therefore, girls aged ten and above were treated the same

in the eyes of the law as an adult woman yet, in the eighteenth
century, society would still have perceived them as children. The
legal discrepancy in relation to girls aged ten to twelve created
further complications in cases of sexual crime. Confusion caused
by the differing age of consent and age regarding forced intercourse led to many men accused of raping girls between ten and
twelve being charged with the misdemeanour of 'assault with
intent to commit a rape', instead of the felony of rape which was
thought much more difficult to prove.[25] Misdemeanours were
tried at the quarter sessions and these provide less detailed information for the historian than can be obtained from the *Old Bailey
Sessions Papers* or *Assize Records*. From the sixteen Old Bailey
cases of child rape, four of those committed against girls aged
between ten and twelve were retried on the lesser charge. The
need to prove non-consent and resistance by a child as young as
ten or eleven rarely succeeded and assailants were often acquitted.

If they were over the age of ten, girls were expected by the court
to have shown the same level of resistance to assault as adult
women. It was anticipated that a girl above the age of ten was
capable of resisting any attempt made on her virginity. Mary
Homewood told the court the distressing story of how she had
tried to push David Scott off her continuously, but that her
attempts had been fruitless due to his superior strength.[26] From
the 1797 trial of John Briant for the rape of Jane Bell it is possible to see how significant it was for young girls to prove that they
had attempted to resist assault.[27] An apothecary called as a
witness in the trial claimed to have examined the child and to
have found marks of violence consistent with trying to resist
being thrown to the floor and ravished. The court would have
known how unlikely it was that a young girl would be capable of
restraining a grown man, but proof of the use of extreme force
was still necessary so that there could be no question of whether
or not the girl had consented to intercourse. There is ample
evidence that young girls below the age of twelve were treated as
women in that they were expected to resist assault and recognise
a man's attempt to deceive them into consenting. At the same time
their youth meant that much of their testimony could be called
into question by the court.

By law, children below the age of twelve were not allowed to
marry or to testify on oath as a witness in a trial. However, these

same children were deemed capable of preventing the advances of a man. The fact that children did not testify on oath was particularly significant in cases where a young girl was the victim of a rape. For the court to believe in the veracity of a testimony it was required that this should be given on oath, otherwise the evidence constituted little more than hearsay. In a trial for rape there were rarely witnesses or conclusive physical evidence. Instead outcomes usually relied upon the word of the victim against that of the accused. It was recognised by the court that if the victim did not testify on oath it was very unlikely her evidence would be believed. The tendency for claims of rape to be distrusted in the eighteenth century made it all the more important that any testimony associated with a trial for this crime was given on oath. The prosecutrix had to convince the court of her ability to understand the meaning of an oath so that her testimony could be sworn. If it could be proved that she realised lying was a sin then she could be heard on oath, regardless of her age. In the trial *R* v. *Davenport* (1796) the victim, Ann Thacker, was questioned in the following manner:

> The judge asked, 'Do you know what will be the consequence of your not telling that which is true upon your oath?' A. 'I should go to a bad place'. Q. 'What do you mean by going to a bad place?' Q. 'Did you ever hear of God Almighty?' A. 'Yes'. Q. 'Do you think he would be pleased or angry with you if you tell that which is false?' A. 'He will be angry with me'. Q. 'And what if you tell truth?' A. 'He will be pleased'. Q. 'Do you fear him?' A. 'Yes'. [She was sworn.][28]

For the story of a child above the age of ten to be given any credibility in a courtroom she was expected to undergo the same treatment as an adult victim on the witness stand. Yet it is evident from the difficulty in obtaining a child's testimony upon oath that it was also recognised that her very young age did create a problem in understanding legal concepts applicable to adults. In the courtroom, therefore, it was common for the innocence that is associated with childhood today to be denied and ignored, while at the same time the expectations of the wider society were much more directed towards the preservation of the sexual ignorance of youth.

Legal jurists recommended that a charge of rape should be

made very soon after the assault was alleged to have taken place in order to give the claim greater credibility.[29] It was very common, however, for long delays to occur before incidents of child rape were reported. Often this was the result of the victim not mentioning the assault and it being discovered at some later date by an adult. Soreness, difficulty in walking or a discharge on clothing or bedding were sometimes the only indication a parent or adult had that a young girl had been violated.[30] Fear lay at the heart of children's attempts at concealment. Mary Matthews told the court during the 1770 trial of Charles Earle that she was afraid that 'if I told anything of it, he would kill me'.[31] Her testimony continues: 'I was afraid to tell my master or mistress for fear of losing my place, and my daddy and mammy beating me.' The words of Mary were those of a young victim expressing the idea that she feared punishment as though she was responsible in some way for having let the assault take place.

The famous words of Sir Matthew Hale regarding the prosecution of rape applied to charges made both by adult women and by children: 'rape is a most detestable crime but it must be remembered that it is an accusation easy to be made, hard to be proved, but harder to be defended by the party accused, though innocent'.[32] The burden of proof lay primarily with the prosecutrix in rape trials. It is widely recognised today, as it was in the eighteenth century, that the character of the victim, more so than that of the defendant, is often brought into question during a trial as a way of discrediting her claim of rape. The destruction of the victim's character was sufficient for the jury to acquit the prisoner of the charge of rape. A witness stated in the 1735 trial of Julian Brown for the rape of eleven-year-old Susan Marshall that 'she [Susan Marshall] said the prisoner had had to do with her to be sure. I asked her why she did not cry out. Because, says she, he gave me a dram of Aniseed and I shall have a pretty Baby of my own to nurse, and that will be better than crying out.'[33] The witness goes on to describe Susan's character as 'impudent' in contrast to the respectability of the accused. That Susan Marshall was portrayed as having encouraged Brown's sexual advances in return for a drink suggested to the court that she was not an innocent, well-behaved child. It was common practice for young girls to be questioned about their relationships with young men. Mary Homewood was cross-examined about her connection with

Moseley, a young man who worked in the dyehouse where David Scott, her alleged assailant, worked.[34] A suggestion was made by the lawyer that Moseley was afflicted with a sexual disease, so that possibly he was responsible for her affliction rather than the accused. However, this line of questioning proved unsuccessful, as Mary denied any knowledge of Moseley. Even in cases where the prosecutrix was below the age of ten questions were asked about the way in which they 'played' with young boys.[35] A growing awareness of the preciousness of childhood can be recognised in the late eighteenth century and yet, at the same time, the young victim on the witness stand was seen as being as likely to have falsified a claim of rape as was her adult counterpart.

Antony Simpson argues that a few highly publicised cases of extortion through the use of claims of rape led to the prevalence of the 'Blackmail Myth' during the eighteenth century, casting doubt on any charge of rape.[36] Little evidence survives to suggest that women did use rape charges for the purposes of blackmail, but a fear that claims were falsified appears to have been prevalent even in cases involving young girls. It is noticeable in the Old Bailey Sessions Papers that out of nearly fifty accusations for child rape the possibility of blackmail as a reason for the charge was mentioned in only three trials. Nevertheless, there remained a very real concern that many of the accusations made were malicious. The defence lawyer challenged Mary Homewood's testimony, suggesting that she had been 'coached' in what to say by her parents as a way of getting David Scott convicted.[37] The defendant claimed that Mary's father had demanded money from him and said that if he left the area then a warrant would not be taken out against him. Mr Homewood told the court that he had wanted to protect Mary from the public shame of a trial and had therefore requested that Scott leave the area and settle his debt at the alehouse, not that he had wanted compensation.

Rape trials involving young victims could become an arena for the family and the defendant to settle outstanding disputes in public rather than merely being concerned with obtaining justice for the child. Cunningham suggests that there was a tendency for parents in the eighteenth century to 'treat children almost as objects testifying to their own status'.[38] Julian Brown claimed in his defence that 'I brought an Action against them [the family of Susan Marshall] in the King's Bench for Scandal and then they indict me for this rape'.[39] Unfortunately, the impact such stories had upon the outcome of the trial cannot be judged. Claims of extortion or of revenge do demonstrate, however, how the agency of the young victim was limited as the verdict of the trial would be influenced by factors other than just her own story.

The unlikelihood of having supporting witnesses for the prosecution in trials for rape meant that expert medical testimony had considerable significance. However, the delay that sometimes occurred in discovering incidents of child rape could lead to a lessening of the impact of testimony by experts. Medical evidence was important in proving that force had been used against the victim, that full penetration had occurred (to constitute the felony of rape) and that in some cases a venereal disease had been passed on. Nevertheless, medical evidence was not deemed as conclusive proof of a rape having taken place, while disagreements between experts sometimes hindered the victim's case. Many medical experts accepted that venereal diseases could be passed on without full intercourse having taken place. Also, it was believed that for a rape to have been committed the hymen needed to have been completely destroyed. Two surgeons, Mr Gilson and Mr Hyman, both argued in 1777 that for the hymen to remain intact penetration must have amounted to less than half an inch, which led to the defendant being found not guilty of rape and tried instead for sexual assault.[40] A legal precedent was established in *R* v. *Russen* (1777) stating that any degree of penetration of the vagina could be used as evidence of rape in association with proof of force even if the hymen remained intact.[41] However, it should be noted that this precedent did not change the issue of penetration until it was written down in statute in 1828.[42]

For the felony of rape to have been committed the court required the complainant to testify that 'emission' had taken place. On the witness stand the girl would be asked if she had 'felt anything come from him' as evidence that full sexual intercourse had occurred.[43] Semen stains on the girl's clothing could support this evidence if witnessed by a parent or medical expert. The court asked Mary Homewood, 'Did you feel anything come from his body into yours?', to which she replied, 'O yes, a good deal; about the evening it came from me very fast'.[44] This statement probably helped to convict David Scott of the felony, but it was unusual for the child's testimony to be so precise. In many other cases the concept of 'emission' was problematic in that it is evident the young witnesses rarely understood what was meant by the question. Ten-year-old Grace Pitts said she saw something wet on the ground but had not felt anything inside her and that Hunter had only entered her a little way.[45] He was later acquitted. The burden of proof in any rape trial made a successful conviction difficult but child complainants faced the further disadvantage of having to understand what was being asked of them in an adult male-dominated environment: the courtroom.

Child witnesses underwent the same ordeal as adults in the courtroom. Today the use of video testimonies and forensic evidence has aided child victims in pursuing their attackers through the courts. During the eighteenth century the distressing nature of cross-examination frequently led to child witnesses becoming upset and confused:

> Prisoner. Q. 'You say I came up to bed to you that Monday morning?' A. 'Yes'. Q. 'You was asleep when I came up?' A. 'Yes'. Q. 'Your Lordship hears what she says; I would be very glad if you would examine her to that; she says, she saw me come up stairs, and she says I waked her'. Court. Q. 'Did you see him come up stairs?' A. 'I did not; I knew nothing of him till I found him upon the bed with me'.[46]

The child would be expected to remember detailed information. Mary Homewood was questioned about the room in which she had been assaulted and how exactly Scott had held her while carrying out the assault.[47] The technical and legal information required under cross-examination could be difficult and distressing enough for an adult victim of sexual crime to recall and no allowance was being made for the age of the child prosecutrix before the court.

The eighteenth-century legal system was not necessarily completely unsympathetic towards claims of child rape. It was rather the case that discrepancies in the law regarding the age of the victim and the difficulties of proof meant that any complainant faced major obstacles when seeking justice. Moreover, juries were reluctant to convict men of the capital crime of rape unless there was unquestionable evidence of guilt. Beattie has noted that problems associated with gaining a conviction for the felony of rape led to many men in the eighteenth century being charged with the lesser crime of attempted rape which carried a maximum two-year prison sentence.[48] In cases of child rape, a trial for the lesser crime of assault with intent to commit a rape meant that the victim faced far less of an ordeal upon the witness stand.

Mary Matthews had contracted a venereal disease after being assaulted by Charles Earle but as her hymen remained intact it was argued that penetration had not occurred and that venereal disease could have been passed on in other ways.[49] Noticeably, the trial report is much shorter, with far less witness testimony: Earle was acquitted of rape, but detained to be tried for assault with intent. In the trial of William Kirk it was claimed that the finger of the accused had passed a venereal disease to seven-year-old Anne Brown.[50] It was further claimed that his disease made him incapable of committing a rape. Anne Brown was not examined on the witness stand and the charge was commuted to one of assault with intent. When the demand for proof of rape was not so great it was possible for the court to have more consideration for the problems a youthful complainant presented in a trial. It is possible that by trying the prisoner for the lesser crime, growing public outrage towards child rape may have been partially appeased. Crucially, with the burden of proof removed from the victim in a trial for the lesser crime it became more likely that the court would return a verdict of guilty against the accused.

Ann Bishop, aged eight, told her mother that 'he [Francis Moulcer] laid her down and did something to her which hurt her very much, but what he did she could not tell, for she turned her head away'.[51] The young age of some of the victims of rape created a problem with their testimonies in that they were unable to clearly describe what had occurred. Ann Bishop was also very confused about when the assault had happened and could not be any more precise than which week it had been. The reliance upon the convincing story of the victim in trials for rape made testimonies problematic when the victim was so young. Another young victim described her assailant as 'being rude with her' but provided no further detail.[52] In such cases where the victim's testimony was so limited in detail the defendant was found not guilty or had the charge commuted to a lesser one. A conviction for rape relied upon convincing physical evidence and a believable testimony from the victim. In cases of child rape more emphasis was placed on the former by the court but in trials where the latter was absent then a guilty verdict would not be returned. The court was unable to make allowances for the young age of these victims and – as with adults – the burden of proof lay very much with the complainant.

Many of the young girls who told their stories in the Old Bailey had difficulty in explaining what had happened to them. Often, they lacked the language with which to describe their experiences. The court advised Mary Homewood that 'you must overcome all shame, and tell us the truth' when she seemed reluctant to describe precisely what had occurred.[53] She went on to say that Scott had hurt her with part of his body but was unable to tell what it was.[54] It is possible that children did not have sufficient awareness of sexual matters. But it also seems likely that it was seen as inappropriate for young girls to discuss issues around sexuality openly in an adult male-dominated environment. By displaying an unwillingness to talk about the assault the child could be perceived as being of a moral, well-behaved disposition and was less likely to be branded as bold and likely to lie. The court required a young girl to display a level of innocence in her testimony so that her story would be regarded as more convincing. This illustrates a paradox for the legal officials in such cases, without sufficient detail of the assault the truth of the child's claim could not be judged, yet the use of explicit language cast doubt upon the girl's good character.

Rape is the only crime where the character of the victim is more influential in the outcome of a trial than the character of the accused. The previous sexual reputation of the woman could be used to judge whether she was likely to have consented to sexual intercourse. Clearly, where the victim was very young and a virgin, she could not be judged in terms of her chastity. However, character witnesses were required to testify to the good, trustworthy behaviour of the child. At the trial of Julian Brown four witnesses are brought forward to depose that the prisoner had an 'honest nature' and that the complainant was 'impudent'.[55] The prosecution then presented two witnesses claiming the girl was 'sober, modest, virtuous' whereas the defendant was 'litigious'. Brown was acquitted as it was claimed that eleven-year-old Susan Marshall had consented to his sexual advances. Due to the rigour of legal procedure in rape trials the court was led to doubt the 'innocence' of a girl as young as eleven. In the same way that middle-class values in the eighteenth-century courtroom placed emphasis upon the character of female victims of rape as a test of the truth of her claim, they tried to shelter children by demanding innocence of sexual knowledge.

A shift towards more 'discreet' sexual language in the eighteenth century affected the testimonies of child victims of rape. Words such as 'cock' – commonly used in children's testimonies to describe the genitals in the early part of the century – became replaced with the more vague 'private parts'.[56] It is not clear how far this censorship was imposed by the clerk of the court. In *R v. Russen* the male genitals are recorded as 'p____ p____' to protect the reader from intimate sexual details. We are left to guess whether 'private parts' had been abbreviated in this way or instead whether the child had used the popular term 'pee place' to describe the penis.[57] This was probably a censorship enforced by the middle-class values of the courtroom rather than a reflection of widespread change in popular language. An ignorance of sexual matters was a requirement to demonstrate the good character of the complainant. This was reflected in the language that the child could use. The child's narrative could show the court that she had feelings of fear and shame regarding the assault if she used a vague, restricted form of language.

An important way in which a rape victim could demonstrate her modesty to the court was to express feelings of shame about the assault. The emotion of shame suggests that the victim blamed herself for not having done more to resist the assault. Child victims were also expected to express this emotion in the courtroom, an expectation which denied the improbability of children being able to prevent an assault committed by an adult male. Much of the suspicion about claims of rape originated from a belief in the difficulty of having sexual intercourse with a woman against her will. In the eighteenth-century courtroom no allowance was made for a child being unable to resist a rape. Feelings of shame suggest that the child was responsible for protecting herself from assault. Noticeably, this contradicts the growing emphasis on the responsibility of parents in protecting their vulnerable children. The distinction between the parents' and the child's own responsibility for her safety coincided with the legal age of consent. When the victim was below the age of ten she would claim feeling scared as a reason for not reporting the assault rather than shame at what had occurred. However, once the girl reached the age of ten it was common for her in her testimony to state that she had not told anyone immediately about the assault because of feeling shame. As has been seen, Mary Homewood's father did not get a warrant against David Scott immediately as he thought 'we could be but disgraced'.[58] Even if the child herself did not state openly that she felt shamed by what had happened, her family would fear public censure as a result of her loss of virtue. Historians have noted that a transition to 'chastity as the essence of natural innocence' occurred during the eighteenth century.[59] Anthony Fletcher demonstrates how chastity and honour became bound together in both literature and advice pamphlets. It can be seen from legal records that the loss of a woman's chastity, even through sexual crime, was sufficient to cast doubts on her honour. For a child to lose her innocence in this way had the same effect, bringing about public criticism and the potential for injury to her own reputation and that of her family.

For a man to be tried on a charge of child rape it was necessary for a prosecution to be brought against him by the family of the victim. It must be asked why families chose to do this. The difficulties in obtaining justice made a successful conviction unlikely, although the fact that a quarter of sexual crimes prosecuted in eighteenth-century England were for child rape suggests that people had some faith in the legal system. Some trials may have taken place as the result of a private disagreement between the defendant and the family of the accused, as was suggested in the trial of Julian Brown.[60] However, the demands for physical evidence meant that it was unlikely that a child could have been used successfully as a pawn in a game of revenge. Mary Homewood's father at first requested the accused to leave the area as a way of protecting the reputation of his family, and it was only when this failed that he chose to pursue David Scott legally.[61] The parents of the young girls who testified at the Old Bailey were seen by the legal system to have failed in their responsibility for protecting their child and could, indeed, have faced criticism for this.

However, if we concentrate too greatly on the role of the parent in cases of child rape there is a risk of ignoring the agency of the victim. The young complainants were used to working in adult environments and although their age meant that they still came under the legal protection of their parents, they were expected to show an awareness of the threat of sexual crime. It was also believed that such girls should have had the ability to attempt to resist an assault. Although their vulnerability was apparent, this was something denied by the courts. A legal paradox identified the age of ten as being the age at which girls could have a degree of choice about consenting to sexual relations. However, the young rape victim on the witness stand was expected to have coped with advances by a male in the manner of an adult woman. The need for evidence of force and resistance extended to child victims as the burden of proof lay with the complainant, regardless of her age. The character of the victim was brought very much into question. The reliability of her story was frequently challenged; as Mr Knapp had pointed out to the court, an eleven-year-old could have 'a very wicked intent at so tender an age'.[62] As no legal distinction was made between the treatment of adult and child victims of rape the young female prosecutrix had to undergo the same ordeal as a mature woman.

Hugh Cunningham has emphasised the recognition in the eighteenth century of childhood as being a separate and distinct phase in life. This in turn led to an increased sensitivity towards the 'idea' of childhood and a connection with innocence.[63] This model needs to be discussed to consider whether the paradoxes that can be seen in the Old Bailey regarding child witnesses in the eighteenth century were influenced by society's attitude about the need to protect the innocence of childhood. He points to the creation of a middle-class ideology of childhood in the eighteenth century. A growing awareness of the role of parenting in the preservation of childhood came to be emphasised in this period. Evidence from newspapers describes how groups of women would mob alleged child rapists outside the courtroom and communities punished such men when they were found innocent by the law.[64] The outrage displayed towards the crime of child rape that is suggested by these public responses would seem to support Cunningham's theory of the growing belief that childhood needed to be protected and innocence maintained. But attacks by mothers on men who were thought to have assaulted children were not new in the eighteenth century. Such newspaper reports demonstrate not only a changing attitude towards children but also reflect the powerful and important role of the 'mother', as has been recently demonstrated by work on family relationships.[65] However, these ideas about childhood could not be reflected in the courtroom where, in trying a case of rape, the legal system was faced with a number of complexities regarding the need for evidence. In fact, an expectation of innocence put the child victim in a very difficult situation.

Changing ideas about the distinct phases of adulthood and childhood were complicated by the way children were treated by society. This point can be most clearly demonstrated in the eighteenth-century courtroom where victims of child rape were expected to have a sufficient level of reason to understand legal procedures and be able to pass on detailed information. The young age of the victim led to an expectation of innocence about sexual matters, but, paradoxically, through losing her virginity she had lost this 'innocence' and was treated as an adult female. If she displayed knowledge of sexual matters at such a young age, the reliability of her testimony could be brought into question. Society had clearly failed in its aim to protect the innocence of youth. In the Old Bailey Sessions Papers 'innocence' had to be denied when a child entered the courtroom as a victim of sexual crime.

Notes

1   *Old Bailey Sessions Papers* [hereafter OBSP], *R* v. *Scott* (1796), 7th Session.
2   S. Brownmiller, *Against Our Will* (London, Bantam Books, 1975), p. 434.
3   A. Clark, *Women's Silence, Men's Violence – Sexual Assault in England 1770–1845* (London, Pandora, 1987), p. 5; A. Simpson, 'Vulnerability and the Age of Female Consent: Legal Innovation and Its Effect on Prosecutions for Rape in Eighteenth Century London', in G. S. Rousseau and R. Porter (eds), *Sexual Underworlds of the Enlightenment* (Manchester, Manchester University Press, 1987), p. 191.
4   P. Ariès, *Centuries of Childhood: A Social History of Family Life* (London, J. Cape, 1962), p. 29; E. Shorter, *The Making of the Modern Family* (London, Collins, 1976), p. 17; L. Stone, *The*

Family, Sex and Marriage (London, Weidenfeld and Nicolson, 1977), p. 24.

5 OBSP, *R* v. *Scott* (1796), 7th Session.
6 A. Simpson, 'Masculinity and Control: The Prosecution of Sex Offences in Eighteenth Century London' (unpublished Ph.D. thesis, New York University, 1984), p. 141.
7 Of 16 trials there were 5 guilty verdicts; 7 acquittals; 4 acquittals to be tried for assault with intent.
8 This distinction is not made by writers such as M. Chaytor, 'Husband(ry): Narratives of Rape in the Seventeenth Century', *Gender and History*, 7:3 (1995), 378–407; J. Barber, '"Stolen Goods": The Sexual Harassment of Female Servants in West Wales during the Nineteenth Century', *Rural History*, 4:2 (1993), 123–36.
9 OBSP, *R* v. *Scott* (1796), 7th Session.
10 OBSP, *R* v. *Earle* (1770), 2nd Session.
11 OBSP, *R* v. *Briant* (1797), 7th Session.
12 OBSP, *R* v. *Scott* (1796), 7th Session; *R* v. *Davenport* (1796), 3rd Session.
13 H. Cunningham, *Children and Childhood in Western Society* (London, Longman, 1995), p. 74; L. Pollock, *Forgotten Children* (Cambridge, Cambridge University Press, 1983), p. 64.
14 OBSP, *R* v. *Davenport* (1796), 3rd Session.
15 OBSP, *R* v. *Scott* (1796), 7th Session.
16 Simpson, 'Vulnerability and the Age of Female Consent', p. 192. Simpson develops the notion of child sexual abuse as an urban problem stemming from increased interest in paedophilic sex. He argues that a belief in the folklore that sexual intercourse with a virgin could cure venereal disease led to the defloration mania. This belief was acknowledged at both a popular level and in the context of the courtroom.
17 OBSP, *R* v. *Scott* (1796), 7th Session.
18 A. S. Taylor, *Medical Jurisprudence* (London, 1854), p. 640. However, none of the accused in the cases I have examined used this myth of how to cure venereal disease as an excuse for their behaviour.
19 Brownmiller, *Against Our Will*, p. 5.
20 OBSP, *R* v. *Scott* (1796), 7th Session.
21 OBSP, *R* v. *Russen* (1777), 8th Session.
22 OBSP, *R* v. *Briant* (1797), 7th Session.
23 3 Ed. I, c. 13 (1275).

24   18 Eliz. I, c. 7 (1575–76).
25   See OBSP, *R* v. Kirk (1754), 5th Session.
26   OBSP, *R* v. *Scott* (1796), 7th Session.
27   OBSP, *R* v. *Briant* (1797), 7th Session.
28   OBSP, *R* v. *Davenport* (1796), 3rd Session.
29   Sir W. Holdsworth, *A History of English Law*, vols III and IV (London, Sweet and Maxwell, 1936–72).
30   OBSP, *R* v. *Senoz* (1741), 4th Session.
31   OBSP, *R* v. *Earle* (1770), 2nd Session.
32   Sir Matthew Hale cited in Blackstone, *Commentaries on the Laws of England*, vol. IV (London, printed for J. Murray, J. Jarvis and J. Fielding, 1803), p. 214.
33   OBSP, *R* v. *Brown* (1735), 8th Session.
34   OBSP, *R* v. *Scott* (1796), 7th Session.
35   OBSP, *R* v. *Earle* (1770), 2nd Session.
36   A. Simpson, 'The "Blackmail Myth" and the Prosecution of Rape and Its Attempt in Eighteenth Century London: The Creation of a Legal Tradition', *Journal of Criminal Law and Criminology*, 77:1 (1986), p. 106.
37   OBSP, *R* v. *Scott* (1796), 7th Session.
38   Cunningham, *Children*, p. 72.
39   OBSP, *R* v. *Brown* (1735), 8th Session.
40   OBSP, *R* v. *Russen* (1777), 8th Session.
41   OBSP, *R* v. *Russen* (1777), 8th Session.
42   9 Geo. IV, c. 31 (1828).
43   OBSP, *R* v. *Hunter* (1747), 4th Session.
44   OBSP, *R* v. *Scott* (1796), 7th Session.
45   OBSP, *R* v. *Hunter* (1747), 4th Session.
46   OBSP, *R* v. *Davenport* (1796), 3rd Session.
47   OBSP, *R* v. *Scott* (1796), 7th Session.
48   J. M. Beattie, *Crime and the Courts in England* (Princeton, Princeton University Press, 1986), p. 130.
49   OBSP, *R* v. *Earle* (1770), 2nd Session.
50   OBSP, *R* v. *Kirk* (1754), 5th Session.
51   OBSP, *R* v. *Moulcer* (1744), 8th Session.
52   OBSP, *R* v. *Gray* (1735), 7th Session.
53   OBSP, *R* v. *Scott* (1796), 7th Session.
54   See Clark, *Women's Silence*, for a discussion of how the low status of the women who claimed to have been raped meant that the authorities would expect them to have some knowledge of sexual matters.

55 OBSP, R v. *Brown* (1735), 8th Session.
56 OBSP, R v. *Slade* (1734), 7th Session; R v. *Briant* (1797), 7th Session.
57 OBSP, R v. *Russen* (1777), 8th Session.
58 OBSP, R v. *Scott* (1796), 7th Session.
59 See A. Fletcher, *Gender, Sex and Subordination in England 1500–1800* (New Haven, Yale University Press, 1995), p. 394.
60 OBSP, R v. *Brown* (1735), 8th Session.
61 OBSP, R v. *Scott* (1796), 7th Session.
62 OBSP, R v. *Scott* (1796), 7th Session.
63 Ariès, *Centuries of Childhood*, p. 75; Cunningham, *Children*, p. 61.
64 The Universal Register, various dates 1785–97.
65 For example, O. Hufton, *The Prospect before Her* (London, HarperCollins, 1997), p. 210–16.

Home, play and street life: causes of, and explanations for, juvenile crime in the early nineteenth century

Following the end of the Napoleonic Wars in 1815 increasing attention was paid to the problem of juvenile offenders.[1] From this period there was apparently a rapid rise in such offending, a rise reflected in the increase of recorded indictable juvenile crime.[2] This increase was accompanied by a snowballing debate into the causes and effects of such crime, and the appropriate treatment for the youthful perpetrators. However, concern with delinquent youth was not a new preoccupation.[3] Prescriptive literature can be found throughout the early modern period dealing with wayward children, as can texts specifically mentioning child/ youth criminality.[4] Nevertheless, the early nineteenth-century discourse arguably represented a turning point in that it pre-empted the far-reaching legislative responses to delinquent youth which were in place by the later nineteenth century.[5] Historical research into these debates has concentrated on the causes of the increase in crime, and on what might be called the state 'invention' or 'creation' of the juvenile delinquent.[6] The main theme of this discourse was the treatment of juvenile offenders – revolving around the debate about the prisons and other secondary punishments. However, another strand of the debate was concerned with the causes of juvenile crime, and more opaquely, with the domestic and social milieu.

The study of working-class children prior to the mid-nineteenth century, when the vast panoply of Victorian bureaucracy became fully functional, is problematic.[7] Compared to the burgeoning literature on children which was to emerge later in the century,

there were few systematic attempts to investigate the domestic
and social lives of such children. Child welfare provision and
initiatives to deal with poor and neglected children did exist. But
when texts turned to discuss the social situations of delinquent
and poor children (often considered as one and the same thing),
representations of familial relations and street activities
conformed to a typology that was shaped by images of corruption, seduction, and venality. For example, in 1846, a Justice of
the Peace, Walter Buchanan, commented on the iniquities of
parents, 'In fact these persons care no more for their offspring
than hyenas for their whelps after they are suckled. Their object
is *to get rid of them as soon as they can*, in order to have all their
gains to squander in gin and debauch.'[8] Similarly in 1840,
William Beaver Neale, commenting on the dangers of street life
and entertainments: 'Towards noon, they may be seen hanging in
groups about the corners of the streets – some eagerly engaged in
playing at pitch and toss, or some other game of chance; others
diverting themselves with foot-racing, and similar sports; and
others again in small knots, concocting some new robbery.'[9]

Thus, whilst the Parliamentary Blue Books, reports of organisations such as the Philanthropic Society, and other contemporary
pamphlets are useful, they offer constructs of the everyday lives of
delinquent children which are heavily loaded in order to present
a picture of uncaring, and often actively corrupting parents.[10]
They portray a street life that was fraught with danger from both
adults and from other children who peopled the streets.
Characteristically, this debate focused overwhelmingly on crime
in London, and consequently on the debilitating effects of metropolitan life, much of which was inevitably lived on the streets.
Whilst this was not a new theme, carrying as it did continuities
from the eighteenth century and earlier, the combination of the
very explicit concentration on juvenile criminals and the sheer
volume of literature produced, was.[11]

Whilst these texts offer a somewhat limited version of the
extra-criminal lives of delinquent children there are sources
extant which enable a more detailed exploration into such
matters. That such sources exist at all is a testament to the
Victorian obsession with causation. Thus a number of interviews
were conducted with juveniles, in Middlesex and Surrey prisons
and houses of correction, as part of the investigations into the

formation of a constabulary police force in England and Wales during the late 1830s.[12] Around the same period a number of interviews were recorded by William Augustus Miles, also under the auspices of the Constabulary Commission, with boys on the juvenile hulk moored at Chatham, the *Euryalus*. The boys interviewed on the *Euryalus* were all aged sixteen and under,[13] and those interviewed in the metropolitan prisons mainly between sixteen and twenty. Since the latter were referring back to their offending behaviour over a substantial period, these interviews are particularly relevant to the present discussion. Two interviews with female reputed thieves also survive.[14] This material can be complemented by supplementary forms of textual evidence such as the accounts of offending to be found in the papers of the Old Bailey Sessions, newspaper accounts, and criminal petitions.[15]

Much of this anecdotal evidence comes from a small number of years, and could thus possibly be regarded as being unrepresentative. Yet this kind of material is so rare as to override any such considerations. Moreover, it is highly likely that the responses of such children to their experiences varied little over the period. Whilst the levels and frequency of offending were possibly out of the ordinary, many of their experiences were common to all juvenile offenders. It is debatable how much, if any, of this material could be said to be the children's own words (which are presented as reported speech). Even though such narratives are from working-class children, caught up in the criminal justice system, the problem of atypicality still exists. Hence, such children had generally run the gamut of the criminal justice system, were ensconced in prison, or else were awaiting transportation. The words of the vast majority of children who passed in front of magistrates and in and out of the penal institutions are irrecoverable.[16]

The first attempt to outline the problem and causes of juvenile crime was the 1816 *Report of the Committee for Investigating the Causes of the Alarming Increase of Juvenile Delinquency in the Metropolis*. This Committee visited around eight hundred delinquent children in Newgate and other prisons. The report gave the following as the principal causes of juvenile crime:

The improper conduct of parents;
The want of education;

The want of suitable employment;

The violation of the Sabbath, and habits of gambling in the public-
streets;

The severity of the criminal code;

The defective state of the police;

The existing system of prison discipline.[17]

Parental neglect, lack of education, lack of religious obser-
vance, too little employment, and too much street life: these
'causes' became a mantra for the vast majority of commentators,
whatever their background or interests. As suggested earlier,
contemporary analysis of the causes of juvenile crime and the
forms offending took were often influenced by popular stereo-
types of crime and current prejudices. Hence, the very poor, who
'infested' the highways and bye-ways of the metropolis, the slums
of St Giles, Seven Dials, Saffron Hill, Westminster, and
Whitechapel, came to be regarded as incapable of innocence.[18]
There was a casual assumption that these, the very poor of
London, were corrupted from birth. The children from these
areas, the product of 'corrupted' and 'hardened' parents, were, as
one contemporary in 1828 noted, 'cradled in iniquity'.[19]

Yet, the reality of such offending behaviour was usually much
more mundane. Opportunity, need, peer pressure, and excitement
all played a role. Few children would have described themselves
as 'professional' criminals, although it is probable that a degree of
organisation and training existed.[20] In the broader work from
which this chapter is drawn causation is considered from a different angle: asking questions about juvenile offenders' own
understanding of their behaviour. Were they driven by poverty, or
by bad parenting? Or by lack of education or religious training,
as the debates suggested? This chapter will focus on the role of the
street, the home, and parenting in the lives and offending behaviour of criminal children.[21]

Play and street life

The children's explanations for their descent into offending were
remarkably consistent – poverty, usually linked to unemployment; temptations, particularly leisure and entertainment; and the
example of other children, some adults and, occasionally, parents.

Not surprisingly there was no mention of lack of religious training; virtue and godliness were not meaningful concepts in the
world-view of the average juvenile offender. Practical and functional skills and attitudes were far more valuable in the culture of
poverty that many of these children inhabited.[22] As might be
expected, peer pressure played a considerable role, particularly in
the context of adolescence and street life.[23] Adolescent male
pastimes were significant in both contemporary understandings
of juvenile crime causation as well as in the children's own narratives of life style.[24] For example, gambling, both on the street and
in public houses, was seen as a precipitant into criminal behaviour. Central to this association of gambling with criminality was
its characteristically group nature. Hence, in the minds of
contemporary commentators, gambling and gang behaviour were
strongly connected. For example, a number of contributors to the
Metropolitan Police Select Committee of 1817 commented on the
seemingly inexorable slide from street activities, such as
gambling, into fully fledged criminal activity. John Fellows,
constable of St Giles and Bloomsbury, was questioned about the
problems of street gambling: '"There is a good deal of gambling
in the streets, is there not?' – 'Yes; particularly of a Sunday.' 'Has
this a very bad effect?' – 'Yes. If it could be suppressed it would
be the means of restoring some of the lads, and make them good
members of society."'[25]
   The movement from gambling to gang and hence to criminality
was implicit in evidence contributed by Joseph Meymott, church
warden of St George's, Southwark, who commented on the
discourse between boys on the street and inmates of the King's
Bench prison, suggesting that some sort of system was being operated between the two sides of the prison walls, 'gangs of boys
standing round the King's Bench Prison wall, under pretence of
catching balls, which are knocked over by persons playing at fives
within, but who are spending most of their time in gambling'.[26]
This association was made much more explicit by William
Crawford of the 1816 Committee, who in his evidence to the
Police Select Committee stated that: 'Street gambling prevails to a
very great extent, and is one of the most formidable agents in
corrupting youth; the school-boy and the apprentice as they walk
the streets are attracted by these gambling parties, and thus
become acquainted with the most desperate characters, whose

society ultimately proves their ruin.'[27]

The evidence of adolescent boys themselves did little to undermine the contemporary perception that gambling, wenching, and visiting penny gaffs (low theatres and public houses) were major pastimes, and a major cause of corruption, although these statements should be read with some caution, taking into account the possibility of bragging and bravado. Sixteen-year-old William Pembroke, interviewed in prison in about 1836, credited his decline into delinquency to 'a particular propensity for tossing and gambling', and to 'drinking, tossing, or larking in public houses'.[28] Experiences of gambling corresponded with the general catalogue of what was seen by authority as anti-social behaviour, but by boys, as very enjoyable. Nineteen-year-old Thomas Keefe, interviewed in the same cohort as William Pembroke referred to his 'irresistible desire for skittle grounds'; yet another, Philip Hall, also aged nineteen, had wanted 'to frequent theatres and to associate with loose females'.[29] For the boys on the *Euryalus* drinking, gambling, and girls had apparently been a common pastime in their former lives: Hewitt 'used to lush hard'; a boy named Walker said of gambling, 'they [the boys] think nothing of that – used to toss for 2*s* 6*d* – the most was a crown'; Henry Thompson, aged sixteen, spent his ill-gotten earnings drinking and gambling.[30]

What is clear from the narratives of the 1830s is that a mixture of motives preceded the movement into criminality. Whilst a few pleaded outright poverty, it was more usual for the children to have some employment, however minor. The indication is that the immediate gratuities of thieving outweighed the merits of honest living. Nevertheless, these descriptions of adolescent street life were fundamentally actions of unruly male youths, rather than specifically of juvenile criminals: hanging around, playing skittles, pitching and tossing, attending the penny gaffs and theatres, and pursuing the opposite sex. Moreover, whilst there were obviously various degrees of involvement in theft (remembering that the child became a juvenile criminal through the mechanism of capture), the boys often described their criminality as part of a general process of delinquency. This could just as well be termed 'adolescent behaviour', characterised by a free and easy attitude, by an aura of excitement, and larking about.[31] The boys themselves used hedonistic language and phrases to refer to their lives. Henry Thompson remarked of the delinquent life style, 'When they once begin they cannot leave it off – because they think it is a very easy life.'[32] This view was confirmed by a twenty-year-old interviewed in 1835 by W. A. Miles: 'It is no wonder boys never reform if they have been in the least success-ful; for look ye here, Sir, the charm of it is, it comes so easy and it goes just as light, it is better than hard work.'[33]

What should be recognised is the role of adolescence, particu-larly the middle teenage years, as a period of extreme vulnerability to delinquency. This was a vulnerability bolstered by environmental factors such as poverty, homelessness, and parental neglect. Most juvenile offenders described their crimi-nality in terms of a conflict between the sorts of peer pressure and youthful behaviour already mentioned, against a background of poverty and disruptive home and work environment. A number of boys and youths referred to fraught domestic environments, with parents often using desperate measures to control their children. Thirteen-year-old Samuel Holmes from Stepney described his enticement into crime: '[I] used to play about in the street, father tried to keep me at home – has stripped me, taken away my clothes and tied me to a bed post – because the boys used to come round the house at night and whistle and entice me to go out thieving again with them.'[34] Francis Boucher, the fifteen-year-old son of a Westminster brothel-keeper, told a similar story:

> Attributes his present situation to the influence of bad boys – who always enticed him to run away, Father used to pay men to bring him back, then he always beat him – severity of his father forced him to run away – Boys used to come about the house to get me out – when father went to the club boys always came for me – used to watch father out of the house because he used to beat any he could catch.[35]

The resort of parents to force to stop their child from offending was not limited to boys. Seventeen-year-old Caroline Gadberry was the daughter of a City officer. Caroline had started shoplift-ing with other girls, telling her parents that she was working late at her employment at a harness-maker in Mile End New Town. She lived a transitory life: in and out of court and penal institu-tions, fencing goods at Field Lane and Petticoat Lane, attending penny theatres and dances, and sometimes going back to her parents. 'During this time she would sometimes visit her parents who would take her clothes from her to endeavour to keep her at home: but she has a great many times run away from them'.[36]

Home

These narratives underline the continual tug-of-war between brutality and desperation on the part of the parents and guardians. It has already been pointed out that parents were, to a large part, held responsible for the delinquencies of their children. Moreover, at times they were accused of taking an active role in the corruption of their offspring. Yet, it is more likely that parental neglect was the culprit, rather than active parental corruption. Neglect was often unintended, a result of trying continuously to balance the scales between poverty and survival. Parents were also subject to the same vagaries of unemployment and underemployment that visited their children.[37] A number of factors undermined familial support. Unemployment, death and disease, poor housing, parental imprisonment: all played their part in undermining the relationship of control between parent and child. However, these reasons contributed to juvenile offend-ing, they did not necessarily cause it, since offenders with a relatively stable and 'respectable' background also existed. For example, one seventeen-year-old identified only as E. L., described the frustrated attempts of his parents to reason with him: 'Father and Mother are working People; they have talked to him about his evil Courses 'till he has almost cried; keeps away from Home, and only sees them occasionally.'[38]

Most juvenile offenders did come from working families. According to a list compiled for the 1835 Select Committee on Gaols, their fathers were employed as bricklayers, labourers, shoemakers, chimney-sweeps, porters, and costermongers; their mothers as servants, laundresses, dressmakers, and needle-women.[39] The compiler noted of the occupations held by parents, 'with respect to the occupation of the father, I beg leave to observe that in very many Instances, the fathers are not journey-men or mechanics, but only assistants or labourers in the Workshops or Manufactories'.[40] Reading the sources it is possi-ble to construct a story where families suffered temporary or permanent unemployment; where the deaths of fathers left widowed mothers; or where the father or mother was in prison or transported. For example, a seventeen-year-old who was on the verge of being sent to the Cape of Good Hope through the auspices of Henry Wilson's School of Industry in Woolwich had lost his father to transportation, on account of his stealing nails to make his son a rabbit hutch.[41] A fourteen-year-old boy had lost his father to imprisonment. His father had been a watchman but had lost his job with the establishment of the Metropolitan Police.[42] Families were cleft apart by death, leaving mothers or fathers to struggle, often with large families. Nine-year-old Nicholas White, one of the boys on board the *Euryalus* in about 1836 had lost his father six years before. As his mother, Mary White, pointed out in petitioning the Home Secretary, 'My Lord I have been a poor widow six years and get my livelihood by honest industry. I am obliged to be out from morning till night and it was during my being at work that my poor child got in company with some evil disposed lads.'[43] Similarly, Mary Bennet, the mother of fifteen-year-old James Bennet, pleaded on behalf of her son who had been sentenced to transportation for life: 'Your petitioner being reduced to want by the death of her husband and by many heavy misfortunes could not engage counsel to defend her unhappy child.' Mary had been hit by a double blow since James had been caught and convicted in the company of another boy, her elder son. 'That accomplice to the further grief of your petitioner is her own elder son – for him she is told she may not ask mercy – she crushes her own heart and is silent in his behalf – but again humbly implores your majesty to commute the severe punishment of her younger boy.'[44]

Bereavement and subsequent marriage were common themes in the early nineteenth century; several children pointed to poor relationships with step-parents as a contributory factor to their delinquency. Information on parentage was compiled by William Augustus Miles from various metropolitan Bridewells and houses of correction. Of 148 children aged under eighteen, 34 per cent had both parents living, 26 per cent a mother living, and 19 per cent a father living. Only 9 per cent had a step-parent (it is not known whether this includes common-law spouses), and 10 per cent were orphans. Finally, one child lived with a stepfather only, and two children had been deserted by their parents.[45] This points tentatively to bereavement as a major factor rather than step-parenthood. Certainly, as evidenced by Mary Bennet and Mary White, the death of a parent could have a deplorable effect on a family's financial situation. Moreover, the lack of discipline and care which may be occasioned by the loss of a parent was underlined by the emotional blow of bereavement. Given the lack of any close textual evidence, the import of family break-up and parental neglect can only ever be conjecture. Whilst such factors are important there were many more factors that might have provoked a child into delinquency. If anything, the statements from boys and youths show the inadvisability of making any crude correlation between parental circumstances/behaviour and juvenile crime.

Whilst most juvenile offenders came from working-class families, there was obviously a wide variety of experience. Moreover, since most discussion of parental experience came either from contemporary commentators or from the children themselves, the construction of family stories/backgrounds has a very distant perspective. In the criminal petitions the voice of the parent can be heard; however, even here information and truthfulness may be being used strategically on behalf of the child. Three main constructions of family experience/background occur. First, a picture of a slightly dysfunctional family, probably a fairly normal circumstance, where drunkenness, or illness, or long-term unemployment had resulted in neglect of the children, often unintentionally. Second, the respectable family, which perhaps again had fallen on hard times, whose child had bowed to peer pressure, or succumbed to temptation from one outside force or another. Third, there was the truly dysfunctional family, much less common, but often favoured in the contemporary discourse – the father and/or mother who actively encouraged their children to thieve; or the parents who abused their children; or the parents who neglected their children's welfare in favour of their own entertainments.

The most marked debilitating factor for many working-class families appears to have been drunkenness. Drink was a major component of the slightly dysfunctional family from which so many juvenile criminals originated. However, there are of course enormous problems with any assessment of juvenile crime, parental culpability, and drink. Given the abstemious leanings of so many contemporary commentators and philanthropists, peti-

tioners were keen to present an agenda of morality and abstinence
as opposed to criminality and drunkenness. It is therefore debatable how factually reliable such accounts were. Of the 32 boys
Miles interviewed, 17 professed to either one or both of their
parents or guardians being drunkards, the other 15 described
parents in reduced but respectable situations: 'has a mother living
who is a tailoress she is a drunkard' (John Anderson, aged 15);
'father and mother living, both weavers and both drunkards'
(James Jones, aged 12); 'father is a currier and his mother is a
washerwoman – both sober' (Phillip Maine, aged 14); 'his father
ran away and his mother is a clog maker – she drinks very hard –
took to it when she lost her husband' (James Edwards, aged 14);
'parents Irish and very industrious people, connected with a
public institution' (George Fitzgerald, aged 16).[46] These statements indicate a wide but troubled variety of experiences. Clearly
drink was a factor, and was constantly seized on by commentators throughout the century. From the earliest Police Select
Committees, through Mayhew, to Rowntree and Booth's surveys
at the end of the century, causal links were made between drink
and crime.[47] However, it is likely that drunkenness was often the
result of indigence rather than indulgence. Many families of juvenile delinquents seem to have been engaged in a fight between
destitution and respectability, and the struggle to keep their heads
above water from day to day. Moreover, most people recognised
that respectability was a major currency and the main selling
point for those parents intent on saving their children from transportation.[48]

Respectability

Parents who wanted, or felt able, to plead on behalf of their children, knew that the best way of doing this was to plead their own
and their child's respectability. Although reduced circumstances
were allowable, a certain gentility permeated such petitions. Most
petitions took the form of a covering letter from the parent or
occasionally the employer, with an annexed list of signatures and
occasionally supporting statements from neighbours, tradesmen,
local clergy, and the like. For example, in the 1835 case of
William Gadbury, who came from a highly respectable family, an
unusual amount of time was spent canvassing good opinions of

William and his family. Inspector Norman of H Division took it upon himself to make a local inquiry about William:

> Mr Joseph Pullen 40 Old Castle Street (a person of considerable property and respectability in the Parish of St. Leonards, Shorditch) states, He has known the Boy from his infancy, he does not recollect his ever being in custody before, that his parents are most respectable, his father is owner of from 40 to 50 houses in that Parish.[49]

Unsurprisingly William's case was being investigated with rare enthusiasm; and, unlike the majority of his contemporaries, William received the reduced sentence of imprisonment in the penitentiary.

Nevertheless, similar devices pleading respectability and enlisting local favour were employed by most petitioners. However, most petitioners had to rely on the words of the local grocer or butcher, rather than of considerable property owners. For example, when fourteen-year-old John Chaplin was sentenced to transportation after being convicted at the Old Bailey at the November session in 1834, his parents Edward and Bridget Chaplin of Bunhill Row, petitioned a number of their neighbours and acquaintances in John's support: 'Chas. Lewico, 25, Sidney Street, Goswell Road, in whose service he was for four months and always conducted himself with propriety'; 'Robert Joyce, Master of the London Society Protestant Charity School, North Street, Moorfields, where he was a scholar for three years, of good behaviour and industrious habits'; 'John Butlin, 16, Goswell Street, has known his father and mother these 12 years to be industrious people.'[50] Most parents determined to seek intercession on behalf of their child used such strategies of deference, of appeals to mercy, of religious righteousness, and of respectability. Only a few were ever successful. Promises of good behaviour, of employment, alternative suggestions such as custody in the penitentiary or a sojourn in the Refuge for the Destitute had little impact on a policy that actively sought to transport juvenile offenders – a policy that was underpinned by a belief in the efficacy of separation and colonial remodelling. The matter of whether or not petitions were a genuine plea seems to have been of little moment to a government administration which was determined on transportation.[51] Certainly, it is probable that poor but respectable parents had brought up a number of these children, and probably they had gone astray in a short time, due to peer pressure, or to detrimental familial or employment circumstances.

There is little real evidence for parental corruption of the type characterised by contemporary rhetoric. Certainly there is evidence for parental brutality, such as that described by Samuel Holmes, Francis Boucher, and Caroline Gadberry, although in these cases it is possible that force was employed in a misguided belief that it was for the child's own good. There were occasional cases of children being tried with parents, often in a partnership of theft and receivership. For example, in 1817 thirteen-year-old John Barnett and his father Lewis Barnett were separately tried; the boy for theft, the father for receiving. The son was found guilty, the father not guilty, denying any relationship to the boy.[52] However, for most parents neglect of their children was unintended, a result of living in debilitating environments, with insecure employment and finances, and often little energy and time to spend on their children.

There were some vicious, malicious parents seeking to get rid of their children by transporting them or imprisoning them. However, these were few and far between. One such parent was the father of fifteen-year-old Henry Wells, who was under sentence of transportation in 1834.[53] Henry was convicted at the October session for stealing from his father a gown which had been the property of his late mother. The mother had died in May, leaving six children to a parent 'whose example, unkindness, and neglect, although they may not extenuate, account in great measure for the misconduct of his child'.[54] The father had quickly remarried and was determined to be rid of the children from his first marriage. According to Henry, he had stolen the gown on the basis of a wish expressed by his mother, who wanted her clothes destroyed in order to stop them coming into the possession of the woman who was to become Henry's step-mother. The author of the letter, Louisa Skeene of 23, Paddington Green, was keen to emphasise the boy's misfortune and the role of his errant parent. Accompanying the letter was a note from William Potter of South Row, Carnaby Market. Potter had employed Henry for two and a half years without complaint. Moreover, 'On the Monday, before he had his trial I went to engage him to come and live with me – again. I saw his father and he declared he would transport him if possible and threatened to turn the elder brother out of doors as he would not support him.'[55]

Another unsympathetic parent was Mr Neal of Archery Ground Cottage, Junction Road, in Paddington, who advertised in the Daily Police Report of 12 June 1837 detailed descriptions of his sons Thomas and James, aged seventeen and fourteen, who had stolen 14s from him.[56] Yet, these stories also possessed broader contexts than parental cruelty and neglect. The father of Henry Wells obviously looked to his own survival, with a new wife and the possibility of a new family to support. The motivation of Mr Neal is untraceable; it is impossible to know whether this was an appeal of care or of cruelty. Finally, most of the parents of these children were poor and harried, caught in the conflict of provision and care of their families and trying to control and prevent the petty delinquencies of their vulnerable, adolescent children.

Conclusion

This chapter has considered the rhetoric of juvenile crime causation through the experiences and commentary of criminal children. Concentrating on home and street life it has argued that the experience of many juvenile offenders was not atypical of the experience of most working children. Limited education, instruction through street life and pastimes, vulnerability in employment, and familial disruption were all familiar pressures in the lives of working-class youths in the early nineteenth century. Where the experience of the children who became offenders differed was that these factors precipitated their entrance into the criminal justice system. Circumstances meant that these factors became significant. Hence, whilst the behaviour and environments described were common to many children, who such children were, where they offended, and when they offended marked the real precipitance into criminality. On the 1852 Committee on Criminal and Destitute Juveniles, there was some recognition of these factors. Captain William J. Williams, Inspector of Prisons for the Home district (London and the south-east), concurred when the following question was put to him: 'Do you not, however, think that children under our present system are often treated

criminally for faults of so slight a character, that if they were
committed by children in any more fortunate state of society, those
children would never be considered as criminals at all?' Williams
answered, 'Many offences are condoned, in the middle and even in
the upper classes, of which we know nothing.'[57]

Notes

1   For example see Select Committees on Police, *Parliamentary Papers*,
    1816, V, 1817, VII, 1818, VIII. For further examples see W. B.
    Sanders, *Juvenile Offenders for a Thousand Years: Selected
    Readings from Anglo-Saxon times to 1900* (Chapel Hill, University
    of North Carolina Press, 1970).
2   P. King and J. Noel, 'The Origins of "the Problem of Juvenile
    Delinquency": The Growth of Juvenile Prosecutions in London in
    the Late Eighteenth and Early Nineteenth Centuries', *Criminal
    Justice History: An International Annual*, 14 (1993), pp. 17–41; H.
    Shore, 'The Social History of Juvenile Crime in Middlesex,
    1790–1850' (unpublished Ph.D. thesis, University of London,
    1996).
3   See particularly P. Griffiths, *Youth and Authority: Formative
    Experience in England, 1560–1640* (Oxford, Clarendon Press,
    1996).
4   Sanders, *Juvenile Offenders*.
5   *1847*: Juvenile Offenders Act (10 & 11 Vict., c. 82). *1854*:
    Reformatory Schools Act (17 & 18 Vict., c. 74); Middlesex
    Industrial Schools Act (Local) (17 & 18 Vict., c. 169); Reformation
    of Youthful Offenders Act (17 & 18 Vict., c. 86). *1855*: Youthful
    Offenders Amendment Act (18 & 19 Vict., c. 87). *1856*:
    Reformatory and Industrial Schools Amendment Act (19 & 20
    Vict., c. 109). *1857*: Industrial Schools Act (20 & 21 Vict., c. 3);
    Reformatory Schools Act (20 & 21 Vict., c. 55).
6   King and Noel, 'Origins'; S. Magarey, 'The Invention of Juvenile
    Delinquency in Early Nineteenth-Century England', *Labour
    History* [Canberra], 34 (1978), 11–27; M. May, 'Innocence and
    Experience: The Evolution of the Concept of Juvenile Delinquency
    in the Mid-Nineteenth Century', *Victorian Studies*, 17:1 (1973),
    7–29; P. Rush, 'The Government of a Generation: The Subject of
    Juvenile Delinquency', *Liverpool Law Review*, 14:1 (1992), 3–43;
    Shore, 'Juvenile Crime'.

7 Anna Davin, *Growing Up Poor: Home, School and Street in London, 1870–1914* (London, Rivers Oram Press, 1996); Louise A. Jackson, 'Family, Community, and the Regulation of Child Sex Abuse: London 1870–1914', ch. 8 below.

8 W. Buchanan, *Remarks on the Causes and State of Juvenile Crime in the Metropolis; with Hints for Preventing Its Increase* (London, 1846), cited in Sanders, *Juvenile Offenders*, p. 191.

9 W. B. Neale, *Juvenile Delinquency in Manchester: Its Causes and History, Its Consequences, and Some Suggestions Concerning Its Cure* (Manchester, 1840), cited in Sanders, *Juvenile Offenders*, p. 170.

10 For example, Select Committees on Police, *Parliamentary Papers*, 1816, V, 1817, VII; W. A. Miles, *Poverty, Mendicity, and Crime*, ed. H. Brandon (London, 1839); Neale, *Juvenile Delinquency;* Philanthropic Society, *First Report of the Philanthropic Society: Instituted in London, September, 1788, for the Prevention of Crimes* (London, c. May 1789); J. Wade, *A Treatise on the Police and Crimes of the Metropolis; especially Juvenile Delinquency, Female Prostitution, Mendicity, Gaming . . . etc* (London, 1829).

11 For example, H. Fielding, *An Enquiry into the Causes of the Late Increase of Robbers . . . etc* (London, 1751); J. Hanway, *Observations on the Causes of the Dissoluteness which reigns among the Lower Classes of the People . . . etc* (London, 1772).

12 Much of this material eventually appeared in the *Report of the Commissioners Appointed to Inquire as to the Best Means of Establishing an Efficient Constabulary Force in the Counties of England and Wales, Parliamentary Papers*, 1839, XII.

13 The actual age of the boys on the *Euryalus* is not always given. Many of these boys can be found on a list compiled by J. H. Capper (the superintendent of the hulks) of boys contained on the hulk in 1835, suggesting that the interviews took place sometime after this, but within a year or two, when the majority would have been transported. Select Committee on Gaols, *Parliamentary Papers*, 1835, 2nd report, XI, pp. 263–6.

14 Public Record Office, London (hereafter PRO), H073/2, H073/16, notebooks 1, 2, 3; H073/16, notebooks, vols III, IV, V; pt. 2, loose papers (for prison interviews, interviews with reputed thieves Caroline Gadberry and Mary Mause).

15 PRO, PCOM 1 – *Old Bailey Sessions Papers* (printed proceedings for the London and Middlesex session, 1801–38); CRIM 10 – *Old*

Bailey Sessions Papers (printed proceedings for the Central Criminal Court from 1834). Of the other records in the PRO, the Petition Archive and Daily Police Reports (1828–38) have been particularly useful: HO 17 and 18, Petition Archive register, HO 19; MEPO 4/12–30. Shore, 'Juvenile Crime', pp. 288–94.

16 The survival of the records of children who appeared at summary proceedings is uneven, making systematic investigation difficult. See R. B. Shoemaker, *Prosecution and Punishment: Petty Crime and the Law in London and Rural Middlesex, c. 1660–1725* (Cambridge, Cambridge University Press, 1991).

17 *Report of the Committee for Investigating the Causes of the Alarming Increase of Juvenile Delinquency in the Metropolis* (London, 1816), pp. 10–11.

18 A typical description of the London slums and their inhabitants can be found in T. Beames, *The Rookeries of London: Past, Present, and Prospective* (London, Thomas Bosworth, 1850).

19 Select Committee on Police, *Parliamentary Papers*, 1828, VI, p. 48, evidence of H. M. Dyer.

20 See H. Shore, 'Cross Coves, Buzzers and General Sorts of Prigs: Juvenile Crime and the Criminal "Underworld" in the Early Nineteenth Century', in *British Journal of Criminology* 39:1 (1999), 10–24.

21 Shore, 'Juvenile Crime'.

22 The 'spiritual neglect' of the people was confirmed by the religious census of 1851. On Sunday, 30 March 1851 no more than 54 per cent of the population of England and Wales aged over ten attended church. G. Best, *Mid-Victorian Britain, 1851–75* (London, 1971; 3rd edn, Fontana, 1985), pp. 196–9.

23 J. R. Gillis, *Youth and History: Tradition and Change in European Age Relations, 1770–Present* (London, Academic Press, 1981), pp. 61–4; J. Springhall, *Coming of Age: Adolescence in Britain 1860–1960* (London, Gill & Macmillan, expanded edn., 1986), pp. 138–47; W. F. Whyte, *Street Corner Society: The Social Structure of an Italian Slum* (London and Chicago, University of Chicago Press, rev. 3rd edn, 1981).

24 For a broader examination of these themes, see H. Shore, 'The Trouble with Boys: Gender and the "Invention" of the Juvenile Offender in the Early Nineteenth Century', in M. Arnot and C. Usborne (eds), *Gender and Crime in Modern Europe* (London, UCL Press, forthcoming).

25 Select Committee on Police, *Parliamentary Papers*, 1817, VII, p. 362.
26 *Ibid.*, p. 492.
27 *Ibid.*, p. 429.
28 PRO, H073/2, pt. 2, loose papers, interview with William Pembroke.
29 PRO, H073/2, pt. 2, loose papers, interviews with Thomas Keefe, aged nineteen, and Philip Hall alias Lovell, aged nineteen.
30 PRO, H073/16, rough notebooks, vol. IV, H. Thompson.
31 Modern biographical investigations of adolescents and of delinquent youth confirm this impression. See P. Willmott, *Adolescent Boys of East London* (London, Routledge & Kegan Paul, 1966), pp. 40, 145; R. Graef, *Living Dangerously: Young Offenders in their Own Words* (London, HarperCollins, 1993).
32 PRO, H073/16, rough notebooks, vol. IV, H. Thompson.
33 PRO, H073/16, Select Committee on Gaols (secret), evidence of W. A. Miles, p. 6.
34 PRO, H073/16, notebook 1, Samuel Holmes.
35 PRO, H073/16, notebook 3, Francis Boucher.
36 PRO, H073/2, pt. 2, loose papers, interview with Caroline Gadberry, reputed thief.
37 For an introductory discussion of the fluctuations of wages and the family economy in this period see M. J. Daunton, *Progress and Poverty: An Economic and Social History of Britain, 1700–1850* (Oxford, Oxford University Press, 1995), pp. 420–46.
38 PRO, H073/16, Select Committee on Gaols (secret), p. 9.
39 These occupations come from tables in appendix 10 of Select Committee on Gaols, *British Parliamentary Papers*, 1835, 4 & 5, XII, 517–25. They are taken from the Bridewell, the several prisons, and houses of correction in the metropolis.
40 *Ibid.*, p. 524.
41 *Ibid.*, p. 449.
42 *Ibid.*, p. 448.
43 PRO, H017/27, Cs/30, petition of Nicholas White.
44 PRO, H017/130, petition of James Bennet.
45 Select Committee on Gaols, *Parliamentary Papers*, 1835, 4 & 5, XII, Appendix 10, pp. 517–25.
46 PRO, H073/16, notebooks 1–3.
47 C. Emsley, *Crime and Society in England, 1750–1900* (London, Longman, 1996), pp. 63, 65, 71; F. M. L. Thompson, *The Rise of*

Respectable Society: A Social History of Victorian Britain, 1830–1900 (London, Fontana, 1988), pp. 319, 329–30.

48   Criminal petitions in the Home Office files in the PRO are a vastly underused source. However V. A. C. Gatrell, *The Hanging Tree: Execution and the English People, 1770–1868* (Oxford, Oxford University Press, 1994), uses them extensively in his discussion of execution and the prerogative of mercy in the late eighteenth and nineteenth centuries.

49   PRO, H017/124, Yr/1, petition of William Gadby (or Gadbury).

50   PRO, H017/120, Xt/3, petition of John Chaplin.

51   The contemporary attitude to the transportation and compulsory emigration of children and youths is discussed in Shore, 'Juvenile Crime', pp. 260–72.

52   *Old Bailey Sessions Papers*, 7th session (1817), no. 1211, pp. 412–13, no. 1344, pp. 448–9.

53   PRO, H017/110, vt/4, petition of Henry Wells.

54   *Ibid.*

55   *Ibid.*

56   PRO, MEPO4/27, Daily Police Report, no. 2936 (Monday, 12 June 1837).

57   Select Committee on Criminal and Destitute Juveniles, *Parliamentary Papers*, 1852, VII, p. 21, evidence of Captain W. J. Williams.

7 *Elizabeth Buettner*

Parent–child separations and colonial careers: the Talbot family correspondence in the 1880s and 1890s

What was the nature of 'typical' middle-class parent–child relationships in late Victorian Britain? Contemporary sources as well as recent historiography suggest divergent ways of perceiving intergenerational affective relations within the nuclear family. Some depict young children born into families with the financial means to employ a staff of household servants as spending most of their early childhood years in the company of maids, nurses, and nannies, seeing their parents mainly at designated and formalised times of the day.[1] When they began their education, many did so under the tutelage of governesses, a course which often preceded a boarding-school education (particularly for boys) when children lived away from their parents for most of the year. In contrast, other accounts emphasise the central role ideologies of family intimacy and domesticity played in middle-class culture, values which permeated other social strata as well.[2] The extent of the disjuncture between widespread ideals and the everyday 'reality' of family life undoubtedly varied according to the individuals in question, and this chapter considers how the members of one British family, the Talbots, conceptualised the differences between their own lived experience and what they perceived to be model family conditions. In this instance, the Talbots' sense of their own inadequacy in comparison with what they envisioned as the norm of domestic intimacy stemmed from the separation of parents and children for years at a time during the course of the father's career spent overseas. The extensive correspondence between Adelbert Talbot and his wife Agnes in

India and their four children who had been sent back to England at early ages chronicles both their disappointment with the family life they led as well as the alternative forms of family relationships they constructed during their many years apart.[3]

British imperial expansion in the nineteenth and twentieth centuries created a wealth of occupational opportunities for Britons from many class backgrounds. For men in particular (along with some women) seeking work which offered social and financial advantages along with the allures of travel and adventure, the empire offered a number of appealing avenues. Some opted for permanent emigration into white settler colonies; others, like Adelbert Talbot, took up appointments which kept them overseas only for the duration of their working life, and continued to look upon Britain as the 'home' to which they returned on furlough and in retirement. The Talbot family correspondence illustrates in striking detail how the lives of parents and children were structured by alternating involvement in metropolitan and colonial arenas. In many respects, the Talbots resembled countless other middle- and upper-middle-class families supported by work in India and other imperial settings during the late nineteenth century. Born in 1845, Adelbert began his career as an Indian Army officer and then moved into the Indian Political Service, in which he served between 1873 and 1900. Agnes Talbot was one of many women who accompanied their husbands overseas in this period. The widespread presence of British wives in India marked a critical shift away from conditions which had prevailed in the eighteenth and early nineteenth centuries, when they were far fewer in number in colonial communities. Although the sex ratio among British expatriates in India remained highly imbalanced throughout the period of colonial rule, more officers, businessmen, and other professionals were encouraged to marry and their wives to remain with them overseas. British wives, many believed, would provide a sanitary and morally upstanding home which would help both to preserve white men's health and to prevent sexual liaisons with native women, as a number of scholars have explored. Inter-racial unions, Ann Stoler argues, were increasingly condemned on the assumption that they destabilised racial and class boundaries between colonising and colonised peoples, thereby weakening European authority over the populations they ruled.[4]

Adelbert and Agnes Talbot's years together in India thus exemplified a form of family life made possible by a combination of middle-class professional opportunities in the empire and the promotion of white domesticity in colonial arenas. Other prevalent colonial practices, however, made domesticity as many Britons understood it necessarily incomplete. Frequent changes of post from one region of India to another prevented the Talbots from establishing a settled household during their time away from their national 'home', as was the case for most families connected with Indian civil or military service. More significantly, methods of childrearing prevalent within the white colonial community resulted in long-term family division when children were sent back to Britain at early ages. Adelbert and Agnes had three daughters and a son born between 1873 and 1880, none of whom remained with them in India past the age of five. This practice derived in part from the dangers India's climate and indigenous peoples were felt to pose to the physical and moral development of white children interacting with them, as well as from parents' reluctance to have their offspring educated in the subcontinent beyond the stage of early lessons conducted at home. Although many 'European schools' existed within India by the late nineteenth century, these maintained a reputation for catering primarily to children of mixed racial ancestry. Given the racial and social stigmas attached to Eurasians, white children as a rule were sent to schools in India only when parents lacked the funds for their journeys to Britain and for educating them upon arrival. If they remained in India beyond a certain age, they risked becoming too closely associated with the mixed-race community and failing to gain the cultural competencies believed to characterise 'respectable' Britons. A family's ability to send children back to Britain consequently served as a marker not only of parental racial and socio-economic standing but also paved the way for the next generation to acquire the coveted attributes which signified genteel status and, in the case of male children, enhanced career prospects following attendance at an English public school.

The colonial childrearing course believed to be the best means of securing class and racial status simultaneously violated cultural ideals of intimacy between parents and children within a sanctified home environment. Letters exchanged between Adelbert and

Agnes Talbot and their eldest child Guendolen during her years at
English boarding schools in the 1880s and 1890s highlight the
centrality of these ideals through their oft-stated regrets at the
divided family life style colonial careers entailed. The Talbots
strove to cultivate on-going family unity despite the distances
separating parents and children and repeatedly looked forward to
the English domestic sphere they hoped to inhabit together upon
Adelbert's retirement. As John Gillis, Paul Thompson, and others
have noted, the field of family history has long been dominated by
efforts to reconstruct the quantifiable families people have, in the
words of Gillis, 'lived with', and not 'the symbolic families, the
family myths, stories, and symbols, they have *lived by*'.[5] Because
the Talbots were forced to communicate their views on family life
in writing by virtue of distance and the frequency with which the
issue arises in their correspondence, their letters provide an in-
depth illustration of the symbolic family they 'lived by', one
which perhaps achieved its importance precisely because it
remained a fantasy, far removed from their everyday reality.[6] In
addition, their letters suggest how families in which parents were
not directly involved in childrearing drew upon a range of surro-
gate guardians in the form of boarding schools and an extended
network of kin.

Given the lengthy periods between parental visits to Britain,
many accounts depicting the condition of children sent 'home'
considered them analogous to orphans for much of their childhood. One missionary society magazine in 1921 described the
offspring of its representatives overseas as 'grass orphans' during
these years of family separation, an assessment equally applicable
to the Talbot children in the late nineteenth century.[7] Although
Agnes Talbot generally returned to England every two years for a
period of several months, Adelbert was restricted by the periods
of official furlough he was allowed, which often meant five-year
intervals between visits with his children. Like many other
parents based in the empire, they were heavily dependent upon
relatives to take in younger children as well as to supervise them
during their boarding-school holidays when they were older.
Their two oldest daughters, Guendolen and Muriel, initially
resided with Agnes's sister and her husband before attending a
small girls' boarding school in the early 1880s. Their aunt prided
herself upon fulfilling her childcare responsibilities with both the

devotion and the duty she deemed necessary for those parted from their parents, writing to Adelbert:

> How strange it seems that the time is drawing to a close for the dear children to leave us! They have found Woolstone thoroughly a home and will always I think have a happy remembrance of these three years – certainly I can conscientiously say that they have been far more anxiously and affectionately watched over than had they been elsewhere ... They fret a good deal at the thought of leaving me at Woolstone, but like all children will settle down in their new life in a few months. Muriel ... scarcely remembers her mother, which must always be the case when separated before five years.[8]

This passage touches upon several of the main themes involved in the recourse to the extended family in lieu of actual parental presence. First, the ideals of providing children with a place they considered 'thoroughly a home' and where they were treated 'affectionately' are stressed, suggesting the significance of these conditions during childhood for both the letter's writer and readers. The tone with which their aunt assessed her three-year commitment to the girls was self-congratulatory, however, implying that she had cared for Guendolen and Muriel as much from a sense of family obligation as from personal fondness. Second, it is also clear that she considered her period *in loco parentis* to have drawn to a close, reminding Adelbert and Agnes that they could depend upon particular family members in only a limited capacity. Thus, while the children's many aunts and uncles as well as their grandparents all performed what anthropologist Micaela di Leonardo has termed 'kin work', none aspired to become permanent parental replacements for the duration of four childhoods.[9] The Talbots consequently turned to an alternating circle of kin in combination with boarding schools to raise their children over the course of more than a decade of separation.

Numerous accounts of British family life split between colony and metropole demonstrate that the Talbots' childrearing dilemmas while living overseas were far from unique. Nupur Chaudhuri and Jose Harris have researched other family papers from this era which detail parents' problems in locating appropriate guardians from outside the family when relatives were not an option, when they might select foster homes from newspaper advertisements without personal knowledge of the prospective

caregivers.[10] The disaster such arrangements might become,
however, was most famously examined and publicised by
Rudyard Kipling, first in his autobiographical short story 'Baa
Baa, Black Sheep' in 1888 and later in his memoir *Something of
Myself*.[11] Kipling's renditions explored the suffering both parents
and children experienced in these circumstances, describing how
he and his younger sister were left as paying boarders with a
woman he called 'Aunty Rosa' in 'Baa Baa, Black Sheep'. The
constant physical and psychological abuse he recalled experiencing in her hands at what he named the 'House of Desolation'
marked a complete contrast to his life in India, surrounded by
friendly servants and loving parents. The memory of being
scorned as 'strangers' children' by his fictive 'aunt' summarised
the extent to which falling outside the bounds of a family circle
characterised by a sense of emotional belonging left its mark upon
Kipling throughout his life.[12] And, though they begged their children not to forget them and were themselves tormented by the
division of the family, the parents in 'Baa Baa, Black Sheep'
unsurprisingly became a rapidly fading memory for this three-
and five-year-old during the five-year separation which followed.

Clearly, Adelbert and Agnes Talbot were comparatively fortunate to find well-intentioned albeit somewhat hesitant relatives to
look after their children before they entered boarding school.
Nonetheless, like the parents in Kipling's accounts, they experienced considerable emotional hardship about missing much of
their childhoods, expressing the anxiety that they would be
forgotten entirely over the course of lengthy separations. The children's aunt's comment that Muriel 'scarcely remembers her
mother, which must always be the case when separated before
five years' touched upon a fear both parents repeatedly voiced in
letters to Guendolen. This appeared to be of particular concern
for Adelbert, whose opportunities to visit were rarer than his
wife's. In several 1883 letters to ten-year-old Guendolen, whom
he had not seen since she left India five years earlier, he told her
how 'it is sad to me to think that I have been away from you now
half your life but I hope to see you some time this year and to have
my little girls to myself again for a few short weeks'.[13] He feared
that 'you must have forgotten Papa quite by this time and will not
know me if I walk into the house some fine day not very many
months hence I hope'.[14] Happily, he was able to visit his children

in England that year; however, following this trip he again had to wait several years before their next reunion. He consoled Guendolen (and, presumably, himself) in later letters that 'we are not much more than three weeks post apart are we?'[15]

Postal communications provided the Talbots with their only means to maintain direct contact and cultivate knowledge of each other's lives. As such, the frequent letters linking them were treasured and viewed as a means of recapturing memories of earlier times together and creating an awareness of their daily lives while apart.[16] Agnes encouraged six-year-old Guendolen in her early efforts to write during her first years in England, stressing that 'I can't tell you how pleased I am to get your letters darling they are my greatest comfort. I like to know that my little girls think of me and remember me now that I am so far away.' Through her writings she strove to enhance those early memories, describing her journey up into the highlands to Mount Abu:

> We came up to Aboo on Monday morning. I was carried up that hill in a chair by four men and Addy sat on my lap. I thought of the day I came up six years ago, when I had a very tiny little baby on my lap, wrapped up in a white shawl. Do you know who that little baby was? ... You must not forget all those nice visits we paid together.[17]

Over the years, parents and children also maintained a frequent exchange of gifts and mementoes, a further means of bolstering relationships and charting the lives of those seldom seen. Guendolen and Muriel received presents from India which included peacock feathers, saris, and bangles, in addition to regular Christmas and birthday gifts; Agnes and Adelbert were able to chart their children's development through inspecting school workbooks as well as drawings and handicrafts sent to them, and looked to the quality of the handwriting and spelling in the children's weekly letters themselves for evidence of how well they were progressing in their education.[18]

Letters thus served not only as a means of exchanging news but were equally important in their capacity as physical evidence of children's growth and well-being. Just as important in this context was the exchange of family photographs, annual updates being anxiously awaited by all concerned.[19] The changes photographs showed their subjects to have undergone could be disturbing, however, particularly the signs that both the children's childhoods were ending and parents ageing more rapidly than expected. Guendolen wrote to her father at the age of seventeen of her parents' most recent picture, '[w]e do not like it on the whole, both of you look so awfully stern ... I think you have both altered a great deal ... I daresay you will find us quite different too. Esmé certainly you will hardly recognise.'[20] Adelbert replied, 'I shall look forward to getting the photographs for I suspect you are all as altered as you think us ... Muriel with her hair up will be a strange creature to look upon as compared with my recollection of her ... of course you are both in long dresses by now, you at any rate.'[21] Although photographs might bring disappointment through the realisation of their lack of familiarity with each other's appearance, they also functioned as icons in their capacity as the closest physical manifestation of those far away. As Guendolen wrote to her mother, 'I kiss your picture (and Papa's too) goodnight and goodmorning'; 'I often look at your picture; when I feel nasty and unhappy I often kiss the whole family round'.[22]

Despite the efforts of Adelbert, Agnes, and Guendolen to cultivate and maintain intimacy through their letters, gifts, and photographs, these methods unsurprisingly proved inadequate substitutes for their actual presence in each other's lives. Guendolen's longing to see her parents was the main theme of many letters, especially those written in the immediate aftermath of their departures from England following furlough. In one letter written from boarding school in 1883 when she was ten years old, she told her mother, 'I do want you so very very much I have no one to tell my things to, no one to comfort me here for of course I can't tell them everything like I would to you. I miss you more than when I was small like last time [you left] but I will try and be happy for your sakes won't I?'[23] The long intervals between visits caused Guendolen to forget what family life was like and simultaneously to long for its resumption. She confessed to her mother in 1884 (several months after their last meeting):

> I feel as if you were kind of locked up toys that one could not have you don't seem to be real out there only a name. You seem like some beautiful thing one caught a glimpse of now and then. I love you *very very* much you know. I have grown quite used to hardly seeing

you now. It seems as ordinary as eating one's dinner. Somehow we are not like other children a bit I don't think. It is almost odd to hear other children talking of their parents as being always with them something too nice for us to enjoy. I seem almost to ache with longing for you. But for your letters and love I should hardly know I had you dear Mama.[24]

This passage and other comments Guendolen wrote to her parents are highly suggestive of the way in which children's writings were dependent upon their gender coupled with the particular setting in which they found themselves in Britain. It is probable, for instance, that Guendolen would not have been in the company of many children 'talking of their parents as being always with them' had she been a boy. As is well known, the tradition of sending boys away from the family to boarding school at young ages was common in many sectors of the British middle and upper classes, but the typical pattern for their sisters was often drastically different. As Carol Dyhouse's work and other scholars' studies of girls' education in late Victorian and Edwardian England point out, substantial numbers of girls never attended schools at all during this era.[25] Many continued to receive all or most of their education in the home or in small, privately run schoolrooms; others who did attend larger institutions run on more formal lines often were sent to day schools rather than away as boarders. This stemmed from parental priorities and economy which caused many to devote the bulk of their children's educational allowance to their sons' schooling, boarding, and career preparation. Most daughters were not specially trained to pursue a paid occupation, however, and they often remained living at home and completed their studies within or in close proximity to their families. This was considered the optimal childhood and adolescent environment for those expected to remain in a domestic setting as adult women. Girls whose parents were in India were much more likely candidates for a lengthy boarding-school education than their socio-economic counterparts from an exclusively metropolitan background. The small schools Guendolen and her sister Muriel attended, for instance, enrolled a combination of boarders – most of whom also had parents overseas – and day pupils living with their families nearby.

For girls like Guendolen Talbot, growing up away from the nuclear family was an aspect of childhood and adolescence heavily dependent upon parents' connections with India; their brothers, on the other hand, might expect to spend long periods of time away at school regardless of their parents' professional milieu. Had Guendolen's younger brother's letters to their parents during his schooldays at Temple Grove and Eton survived as well, this would have enabled a comparison between male and female children's ways of expressing family sentiments, if indeed he chose to do so. In its incomplete state, the Talbots' correspondence indicates how strongly the ideals of family domesticity had been inculcated in a girl at a fairly young age; her brother's perceptions of the way in which the family deviated from these models during the course of upper-middle-class male socialisation may well have taken a very different cast. Adult men's recollections of childhood after being sent back from India, of which Kipling's was only the best known, suggest that many shared Guendolen's sense of pain and disappointment with respect to the lack of direct contact with their parents, at least retrospectively. *During* childhood and adolescence at public schools which commonly promoted stoicism and homosocial group values in opposition to those of the sentimentalised family and domestic sphere, however, boys may not have expressed – or even conceptualised – their experiences and feelings as girls would have done.[26]

Occasions when boarding-school pupils whose parents lived in Britain returned home for the holidays were among those Guendolen found most distressing. As Gillis has argued, by the late nineteenth century holidays had become the most symbolic occasions on which middle-class families celebrated idealised conceptions of themselves, with most holiday rituals now focused on family gatherings rather than on a wider social community.[27] Christmas and summertime travels were occasions that most children experienced in a family setting, regardless of the months they may have spent away at school. Because most of the Talbots' relations were not able or willing to accommodate four siblings at once during school holidays, Guendolen and Muriel rarely saw their younger brother Addy and sister Esmé. Thus, even contacts with nuclear family members in England were circumscribed. One low point occurred in 1888 when all four children were united during the summer holidays but supervised by the three unmarried sisters – the 'Miss Coopers' – who ran Guendolen and Muriel's boarding school. Describing their month-long stay at Brighton to her mother, Guendolen wrote:

> The holidays seem so horrid without you and Papa, we seem so lonely, for though I suppose [the Coopers] mean to be kind . . . one is always obliged to have one's company manners on with them, and you can't get any further . . . [Addy] hates the Coopers, and no wonder for they are a set of old fogeys . . . They don't give us holiday food at all it is just like being at school, and they don't trouble much to amuse us . . . If the Coopers promise to take you anywhere, they generally forget or else purposely don't do it.[28]

These periods of prolonged separation caused Agnes and Adelbert Talbot to comfort themselves as well as their children in letters by making plans for their future happiness when all were together in England. Agnes wrote to Guendolen in 1889, 'I used to be so fond of building castles in the air when I was a girl and I have the same inclination now in a way, but what I think of is how to furnish comfortably and prettily a small house in which Papa and I can spend the rest of our lives [with] you all I hope for some years and years'.[29] Guendolen helped her parents to enhance this dream, writing to her father, '[t]his night last year was Mama's last night with us, I remember it well, but you will both be coming home in a year or less now won't you? How delightful it will be for us to be all together again; Mama and I used to make castles in the air about it often, of how we should like our house to be.'[30] Over the course of years of letters, the Talbots collectively envisioned a future when Adelbert and Agnes's 'coming home' to England would mean, first temporarily during furlough and then permanently in retirement, establishing a household where parents and children would all live together. For many years, however, their dream of 'home' – with its double connotation of familial domestic sphere and national homeland – had to remain no more than a fantasy, a 'castle in the air'.

As Adelbert entered his final years in the Indian Political Service in the 1890s, the family made more concrete plans for his retirement. First, Agnes left India permanently to settle in England after Guendolen and Muriel completed their schooling, and Adelbert eagerly awaited the chance to join them in their new

household when his career ended. Having long since tired of life
in India and frequent changes of post, he seemed equally capti-
vated by an ideal of domesticity as his wife and daughter. He
looked forward to an English garden he and Agnes could call
their own and enjoyed the notion of soon owning a full comple-
ment of household furnishings for the first time. Leonore
Davidoff, Jeanne L'Esperance, and Howard Newby have
suggested that English middle-class ideals of home were closely
related to concepts of an English rural idyll, noting the particular
potency this combined imagery might have for those living
abroad. Their assertion that '[o]verseas expansion, too, made
images of Home amidst the green surroundings of the English
village a particularly compelling ideal' is well supported by attitudes conveyed throughout the Talbots' letters.[31]

The Talbots set up a household outside Tunbridge Wells, but
their dreams of English domesticity, permanency, and family
unity were soon shattered, however, by Agnes's untimely death
after a brief illness in 1894. This misfortune disrupted all the
family's carefully laid plans for their future when, as Adelbert had
written, 'we should all be together for good'.[32] Adelbert remained
in India for another six years before retiring in 1900, but upon his
final return 'home' none of his grown children were there to greet
him. Within several years of their mother's death all three daughters had joined him in India, despite his initial efforts to dissuade
them from coming. He predicted – accurately, as it turned out –
that they, like so many daughters returning to their parents in
India, might marry and remain there through most of their adulthood, thus replicating the family's pattern of residence away from
'home' he deeply regretted.[33] He wrote to Guendolen,

> Your mother and I hoped that you would none of you come out to
> India, but if you wish to do so I will not stand in the way.
> Remember that an Indian life is a hard one for women in many
> ways. You know what it has meant in our case, and how we have
> been practically exiles, with many separations from those we love
> ... You must weigh against this [the] prospect of a quiet life at
> Frant in our own little home, in your own country with Addy and
> Esmé.[34]

Despite his oft-stated misgivings about British colonial life, his
guidance to his children was always contradictory with respect to

its advantages and disadvantages. He not only allowed his daughters to come but also successfully encouraged his son Addy to join the Indian Civil Service.[35] Like many, he retained sufficient confidence that the East remained a promising setting in which to make a career. In addition, family traumas concerning separations were not enough to prevent many grown children from viewing India as glamorous or adventurous and from desiring to experience the empire's perceived attractions for themselves. Adelbert wrote to Guendolen from his post with the Foreign Office at Simla that Muriel 'constantly writes extolling Simla, and if I stay here would no doubt insist on coming out, for nothing I could say I fear would dissuade her from the belief that Simla is an Earthly Paradise'.[36] All three of his daughters chose to marry and stay in India after his retirement, Guendolen and Esmé both having met their future husbands among his junior colleagues in the Indian Political Service. For the Talbots and many others, a family identity characterised by parent–child separations and 'homelessness' was perpetuated across the generations in large part because family conditions encouraged its replication, despite the concomitant dissatisfactions colonial life entailed. Later correspondence between Muriel and her husband and their daughter after she was sent to an English boarding school during the 1920s showed the same family difficulties in coping with separations as had existed between the Talbot children and their parents.[37]

Adelbert's dreams of domesticity with his family in England were therefore limited to seeing his adult children during their short visits on furlough and to supervising his grandchildren during many of their school holidays once they left India for English boarding schools. Until his death in 1920, he was able to share in his grandchildren's childhoods in a manner unlike that which had been logistically possible with his own son and daughters. Like his children's aunts, uncles, and grandparents had done in earlier years, he acquired an important role through engaging in the 'kin work' which actively structured the childhoods of the next generation of his colonial descendants. In his family, childhood continued to be a period of life when other family members played a more direct role than parents, diverging from the path widely deemed most conducive to happiness. For the sector of the middle classes choosing careers in the empire, the childrearing

practices many followed constituted an uneasy deviation from the
culturally and psychologically pervasive imagery of idyllic family
unity and models of proper childhood and parenthood.

Notes

1 Leonore Davidoff, 'Class and Gender in Victorian England: The
   Case of Hannah Cullwick and A. J. Munby', in *Worlds Between:
   Historical Perspectives on Gender and Class* (New York,
   Routledge, 1995), p. 109; Carol Dyhouse, 'Mothers and Daughters
   in the Middle-Class Home, c. 1870–1914', in Jane Lewis (ed.),
   *Labour and Love: Women's Experiences of Home and Family,
   1850–1940* (Oxford, Basil Blackwell, 1986), pp. 28–9; Jonathan
   Gathorne-Hardy, *The Rise and Fall of the British Nanny* (London,
   Hodder & Stoughton, 1972); Peter Stallybrass and Allon White,
   'Below Stairs: The Maid and the Family Romance', in *The Politics
   and Poetics of Transgression* (Ithaca, N.Y., Cornell University
   Press, 1986), pp. 149–70. In less affluent middle-class families
   employing only one or two domestic servants, mothers were more
   likely to perform a wider range of childcare duties than women with
   larger and more specialised household staffs.
2 Leonore Davidoff and Catherine Hall, *Family Fortunes: Men and
   Women of the English Middle Class, 1780–1850* (Chicago,
   University of Chicago Press, 1987); John R. Gillis, 'Ritualization of
   Middle-Class Family Life in Nineteenth-Century Britain',
   International Journal of Politics, Culture, and Society, 3:2 (1989),
   213–35; and *A World of Their Own Making: Myth, Ritual, and the
   Quest for Family Values* (New York, Basic Books, 1996). See also
   Sonya O. Rose, *Limited Livelihoods: Gender and Class in
   Nineteenth-Century England* (Berkeley, University of California
   Press, 1992); Ellen Ross, *Love and Toil: Motherhood in Outcast
   London, 1870–1918* (Oxford, Oxford University Press, 1993);
   Anna Clark, 'The Rhetoric of Chartist Domesticity: Gender,
   Language, and Class in the 1830s and 1840s', *Journal of British
   Studies*, 31 (1992), 62–88, for discussions of the importance the
   British working classes also placed upon particular models of
   domesticity and family relations.
3 The Talbots' letters form part of the Godfrey Collection of the
   British Library's Oriental and India Office Collections (hereafter
   OIOC), MSS.Eur.E.410.

4   Ann Laura Stoler, 'Carnal Knowledge and Imperial Power:
    Gender, Race, and Morality in Colonial Asia', in Micaela di
    Leonardo (ed.), *Gender at the Crossroads of Knowledge: Feminist
    Anthropology in a Postmodern Era* (Berkeley, University of
    California Press, 1991), pp. 55–101; 'Rethinking Colonial
    Categories: European Communities and the Boundaries of Rule',
    Comparative Studies in Society and History, 31:1 (1989), 134–61;
    *Race and the Education of Desire: Foucault's History of Sexuality
    and the Colonial Order of Things* (Durham, N.C., Duke
    University Press, 1995). Among the many studies delineating
    European women's presence and role in the colonies, see Helen
    Callaway, *Gender, Culture, and Empire: European Women in
    Colonial Nigeria* (London, Macmillan, 1987); Rosemary
    Marangoly George, 'Homes in the Empire, Empires in the Home',
    Cultural Critique (Winter 1993–94), 95–127; Nupur Chaudhuri,
    'Memsahibs and Motherhood in Nineteenth-Century Colonial
    India', *Victorian Studies*, 31:4 (1988), 517–35; Claudia Knapman,
    White Women in Fiji, 1835–1930: The Ruin of Empire? (Sydney,
    Allen & Unwin, 1986); Margaret Strobel, *European Women and
    the Second British Empire* (Bloomington, Indiana University Press,
    1991); Nupur Chaudhuri and Margaret Strobel (eds), *Western
    Women and Imperialism: Complicity and Resistance*
    (Bloomington, Indiana University Press, 1992); Dane Kennedy,
    *Islands of White: Settler Society and Culture in Kenya and
    Southern Rhodesia, 1890–1939* (Durham, N.C., Duke University
    Press, 1987); Hilary Callan and Shirley Ardener (eds), *The
    Incorporated Wife* (London, Croom Helm, 1984).
5   John R. Gillis, 'Making Time for Family: The Invention of Family
    Time(s) and the Reinvention of Family History', *Journal of Family
    History*, 21:1 (1996), p. 7; see also his 'Ritualization of Middle-
    Class Family Life' and *A World of Their Own Making*, as well as
    Paul Thompson, 'Family Myth, Models, and Denials in the Shaping
    of Individual Life Paths', in Daniel Bertaux and Paul Thompson
    (eds), *International Yearbook of Oral History and Life Stories*, vol.
    II: *Between Generations: Family Models, Myths, and Memories*
    (Oxford, Oxford University Press, 1993), pp. 13–38; Raphael
    Samuel and Paul Thompson (eds), *The Myths We Live By* (London,
    Routledge, 1990); Tamara Hareven, 'Recent Research on the
    History of the Family', in Michael Drake (ed.), *Time, Family and
    Community: Perspectives on Family and Community History*

(Oxford, Oxford University Press in association with Blackwell, 1994), pp. 13–43.

6 John Tosh similarly notes how the stresses of physical separation and geographical mobility prompted families to 'articulate so much that they normally took for granted' in letters which thereby provide 'insight into . . . priorities,' in 'From Keighley to St-Denis: Separation and Intimacy in Victorian Bourgeois Marriage', *History Workshop Journal*, 40 (1995), 204–5.

7 *Outward Bound* (Jan. 1921), 299.

8 OIOC, MSS.Eur.E.410/65, Mary Coventry to Adelbert Talbot, 15 Dec. [n. d., c. 1880].

9 See Micaela di Leonardo, 'The Female World of Cards and Holidays: Women, Families, and the Work of Kinship', *Signs: A Journal of Women in Culture and Society*, 12:3 (1987), 440–53, for an illuminating exploration of women's 'kin work' in maintaining extended family relations through perpetuating activities such as holiday celebrations, visits and letters, and sharing other family responsibilities.

10 Chaudhuri, 'Memsahibs and motherhood', 533–5; Jose Harris, *Private Lives, Public Spirit: Britain, 1870–1914* (Harmondsworth, Penguin, 1994), p. 82, and *William Beveridge: A Biography* (Oxford, Oxford University Press, 1977).

11 Rudyard Kipling, *Something of Myself* and 'Baa Baa, Black Sheep', in Thomas Pinney (ed.), *Rudyard Kipling: Something of Myself and Other Autobiographical Writings* (Cambridge, Cambridge University Press, 1990), pp. 5–10, 137–64.

12 Kipling not only echoed his contemporaries but also inspired many later writers to depict their own childhoods using his work as a paradigm. Among the many late twentieth-century autobiographers who frame their colonial childhood experiences with explicit reference to Kipling's renditions, see Alan Ross, *Blindfold Games* (London, Collins Harvill, 1986), pp. 68–9, and M. M. Kaye, *The Sun in the Morning: My Early Years in India and England* (New York, St. Martin's Press, 1990), pp. 369, 379.

13 OIOC, MSS.Eur.E.410/6, Adelbert Talbot to Guendolen Talbot, 20 Jan. 1883.

14 *Ibid.*, Adelbert Talbot to Guendolen Talbot, 9 Jan. 1883.

15 *Ibid.*, Adelbert Talbot to Guendolen Talbot, 30 May 1884.

16 On the rituals involved in colonial family letter-writing and its functions in a Danish missionary family divided between Denmark and

South India, see Poul Pedersen, 'Anxious Lives and Letters: Family Separation, Communication Networks and Structures of Everyday Life', *Culture and History*, 8 (1990), 7–19.

17 OIOC, MSS.Eur.E.410/21, Agnes Talbot to Guendolen Talbot, 15 March [1879].

18 OIOC, MSS.Eur.E.410/4, Adelbert Talbot to Guendolen Talbot, 5 July 1889; MSS.Eur.E.410/1, Adelbert Talbot to 'My dear children', 5 Dec. 1882; MSS.Eur.E.410/21, Agnes Talbot to Guendolen Talbot, 6 Nov. [n. d.]; 18 Nov. [n. d.]; 7 July [n d.]; MSS.Eur.E.410/27, Agnes Talbot to Guendolen Talbot, 19 Oct. 1889; MSS.Eur.E.410/34, Guendolen Talbot to Adelbert Talbot, 24 May 1884; MSS.Eur.E.410/32, Guendolen Talbot to Adelbert Talbot, 29 June [n. d.]; MSS.Eur.E.410/8, Adelbert Talbot to Guendolen Talbot, 5 Jan. 1895.

19 OIOC, MSS.Eur.E.410/1, Adelbert Talbot to Guendolen Talbot, 20 May 1880; 17 May 1881.

20 OIOC, MSS.Eur.E.410/38, Guendolen Talbot to Adelbert Talbot, 28 Aug. 1890.

21 OIOC, MSS.Eur.E.410/4, Adelbert Talbot to Guendolen Talbot, 21 Sept. 1890.

22 OIOC, MSS.Eur.E.410/33, Guendolen Talbot to Agnes Talbot, 26 Nov. 1883; 2 Dec. 1883.

23 *Ibid.*, Guendolen Talbot to Agnes Talbot, 2 Dec. 1883.

24 OIOC, MSS.Eur.E.410/34, Guendolen Talbot to Agnes Talbot, 2 March 1884.

25 Carol Dyhouse, *Girls Growing Up in Late Victorian and Edwardian England* (London, Routledge & Kegan Paul, 1981), pp. 3, 41; and 'Mothers and Daughters in the Middle-Class Home'. Also see Deborah Gorham, *The Victorian Girl and the Feminine Ideal* (Bloomington, Indiana University Press, 1982), pp. 20–2, 73–5; Joan N. Burstyn, *Victorian Education and the Ideal of Womanhood* (London, 1980); M. Jeanne Peterson, *Family, Love, and Work in the Lives of Victorian Gentlewomen* (Bloomington, Indiana University Press, 1989), pp. 35–57; Pat Jalland, *Women, Marriage and Politics 1860–1914* (Oxford, Clarendon Press, 1986), pp. 10–17; Barbara Caine, *Destined to be Wives: The Sisters of Beatrice Webb* (Oxford, Clarendon Press, 1986), pp. 43–50.

26 J. R. de S. Honey, *Tom Brown's Universe: The Development of the Victorian Public School* (London, Millington, 1977), pp. 204–5.

27 Gillis, *A World of Their Own Making*, pp. 98–107. See also Anne

Martin-Fugier, 'Bourgeois rituals', in Michelle Perrot (ed.), Arthur Goldhammer (trans.), *A History of Private Life,* vol. IV: *From the Fires of Revolution to the Great War* (Cambridge, Mass., Belknap/Harvard University Press, 1990), pp. 285–307, for a discussion of bourgeois French society which suggests similarities between British and other west European middle-class family cultures.

28 OIOC, MSS.Eur.E.410/36, Guendolen Talbot to Agnes Talbot, 5 Aug. 1888; MSS.Eur.E.410/30, Guendolen Talbot to Agnes Talbot, 19 Aug. [1888].

29 OIOC, MSS.Eur.E.410/27, Agnes Talbot to Guendolen Talbot, 22 Aug. 1889.

30 OIOC, MSS.Eur.E.410/33, Guendolen Talbot to Adelbert Talbot, 23 Nov. [n. d., c. 1884].

31 Leonore Davidoff, Jeanne L'Esperance, and Howard Newby, 'Landscape with Figures: Home and Community in English Society', in Davidoff, *Worlds Between,* p. 43.

32 OIOC, MSS.Eur.E.410/7, Adelbert Talbot to Guendolen Talbot, 8 Sept. 1894.

33 Maud Diver's widely read account, *The Englishwoman in India* (Edinburgh and London, William Blackwood & Sons, 1909), asserted that 'more than half of the [married] Englishwomen in India today have spent their girlhood and early childhood in the country itself, which, in most cases, means that they have been sent 'Home' at the age of seven or thereabouts, returning at seventeen', p. 11.

34 OIOC, MSS.Eur.E.410/7, Adelbert Talbot to Guendolen Talbot, 18 Oct. 1894.

35 For the particulars of Adelbert Talbot's and his son's careers in India, see *The India Office List for 1907* (London, Harrison & Sons, 1907), p. 643.

36 OIOC, MSS.Eur.E.410/7, Adelbert Talbot to Guendolen Talbot, 25 Aug. 1894; see also MSS.Eur.E.354/36, Esmé Talbot to Muriel Talbot, 19 Feb. [1896].

37 See OIOC, MSS.Eur.E.354/28, letters to Muriel Brown from Barbara Brown, c. 1924–31, and MSS.Eur.E.354/29, letters to Muriel and Percy Brown from Barbara Brown, 1922–23, along with many other files of family correspondence in the Brown Collection.

Family, community and the regulation of child sexual abuse: London, 1870–1914

In July 1870 an Islington mother told magistrates at Clerkenwell Police Court how she had confronted a male lodger for molesting her six-year-old daughter: 'He said "Well don't lock me up, don't lock me up, I'll pay any expenses and I'll never touch anyone again". I said "I must lock you up for the sake of other poor children".'[1] Legal depositions, such as the one in which these words are recorded, provide striking insights on attitudes to family, community and moral regulation. They contain vivid stories of the lives of ordinary Londoners with details of the everyday and the particular, information about the relationships of parent and child, friends or neighbours, and indications of attitudes to professionals and figures ostensibly in authority. They do, furthermore, provide insights which counter previous attempts by historians to explain nineteenth-century attitudes towards child sexual abuse.

Most historical accounts have focused on the way sexual abuse and incest were represented by middle-class officials, journalists and social-purity reformers. Numerous parliamentary and local-government reports had described the poor as desensitised to immorality, close living conditions precluding any possession of honour or shame. In *The Bitter Cry of Outcast London*, the Rev. Andrew Mearns had argued that 'incest is common; and no form of vice and sensuality causes surprise or attracts attention'.[2] The 1885 Royal Commission on the Housing of the Working Classes had reported to Parliament that the system by which whole families lived in one room, due to the high rate of rents in the

Metropolis, was both physically and morally detrimental.[3] Anthony Wohl's 1978 essay, which took the accounts of these reformers at face value, arguing that incest probably was accepted amongst the poor, is long due for overhaul.[4] As Anna Davin has commented, 'it is not safe to infer from overcrowding that family relationships were warped or diminished'.[5]

In contrast to Wohl, Judith Walkowitz has examined how newspaper editor W. T. Stead manipulated and mobilised class prejudices in his exposé of juvenile prostitution, 'The Maiden Tribute of Modern Babylon', published in the *Pall Mall Gazette* in July 1885.[6] She has demonstrated how the traditional melodramatic figure of the aristocratic rake who seduced and defiled the daughters of the poor was used to harness working-class support for the campaign for a Criminal Law Amendment Act to raise the age of consent for girls from thirteen to sixteen. The focus, however, remains on Stead's text and on middle-class interventions in popular culture.

The situation which can be glimpsed by examining proceedings in London's courts of law was very different from the emphases of either Andrew Mearns or W. T. Stead: the poor were clearly not desensitised to abuse against their children, but, when forced to confront abuse, it was invariably from within their neighbourhoods rather than from any aristocratic impostor. The majority of abuse cases which came into the London courts involved working-class complainants and defendants. It is important to stress that depositions, shaped as they were by the questions of police officers, lawyers, and judges, raise problems in terms of authorial voice. The courts required the production of a narrative which was structured and coded in relation to existing scripts. Care must be taken in treating depositions simply as a verbatim report of a witness's original story. However, as Natalie Davis has commented in her work on sixteenth-century French legal sources, depositions can be 'valuable indicators of the way people recounted events';[7] they do tell us a great deal about how people reacted to moments of crisis and made sense of experiences. Court depositions form a largely untapped source which can provide a great deal of information about the daily lives of the lower classes and about strategies of sexual regulation. It is clear from these testaments that parents, friends and relations in various working-class neighbourhoods viewed the abuser in relation to a set of common cultural, social and moral codes, and that witnesses were very clear about the strategies which could or should be taken.

This chapter is based on a study sample of over 900 sexual assault and rape cases which came before London magistrates, quarter-sessions courts and the Central Criminal Court at the Old Bailey in the period 1870–1914, of which an estimated three-quarters involved child victims.[8] It will argue that recourse to the law was more likely to result in cases involving extra-familial abuse; alternative forms of shaming and ostracisation were deployed in cases involving incest. While without doubt a large number (and possibly the majority) of incidents of sexual abuse remained secret and hidden, it is important to recognise that this was not uniformly the case; sexual abuse was discussed, problematised and reported. Court depositions allow us to examine the circumstances which affected this reporting; they also shed light, as I shall demonstrate, on structures of power, based on age and gender, in the Victorian family.

Community regulation of extra-familial abuse

Forming a focal point of the witness's narrative, the confrontation between abuser and parent (or another adult *in loco parentis*) revealed popular perceptions of the abuser in Victorian society. This moment of tension was the point where the knowing and therefore empowered adult (rather than the innocent and hence powerless child) had the chance to tell the abuser what s/he thought of him, to strike out verbally if not physically. The immediate reaction of adult witnesses seems to have been one of shock and horror, articulated through a common vocabulary of insult which identified the abuser in terms of dirt, evil and bestiality: 'Dirty old man'; 'You vagabond, I'll kill you'; 'You dirty beast'; 'Old beast'; 'What a wicked thing for an old wretch like you to do to a baby'; 'You beastly man'; 'Dirty pig'; 'Dirty goat'.[9] We can sense in these written exclamations the condemnation, the raised intonation and the shocked tone of voice. As Judith Irvine has written, in an anthropological study of insult and defamation, verbal insults 'involve evaluative statements grounded in specific cultural systems of moral judgment'.[10] Insults, such as those quoted here, not only referred to specific moral codes, but, indeed, served repeatedly to re-establish and demarcate that moral order. Moral deviance was articulated in terms of physical deformity and monstrosity. The abuser was commonly seen as unclean, unhuman and inhumane, a monster or hybrid, who, as such, was outside the boundaries of civilised human society. As a 'beast', the abuser was to be cordoned off from humanity; removal from the community was seen as requisite in order to 'protect the children' (as the Islington mother put it).

The stereotype of the sexual 'beast' was a familiar one in the nineteenth century. Walkowitz has described how much of the rhetoric of Stead's 'Maiden Tribute' articles, which created the image of a minotaur stalking London in search of young virgins to satisfy its carnal lusts, was drawn from popular domestic melodrama and the newer form of the gothic fairy tale.[11] The language of bestiality which was used by Stead with much self-conscious literary and mythical referencing also resonated quite audibly with the language of the street, as well as with concerns and issues which were expressed there long before 1885.

Parents, relations and neighbours played key roles, which were frequently gender-related, in discovering and reporting incidents of child sexual abuse. Mothers, as Ellen Ross has so carefully detailed, were the central figures responsible for family survival in London's working-class communities; as feeders and primary carers, they were the 'guardians of children's bodies'.[12] Since they were usually responsible for dressing a child and doing the laundry, they were quick to notice signs of abuse. Time and time again they spotted stains on bedclothes, knickers or chemises: 'I'd seen some marks on her linen, & the child was queer – mopish. I'd fathomed it out a little at a time ... I kept looking, thinking to be sure it was so – It was four weeks ago I was certain what I saw was the marks of a man.'[13] A mother then proceeded to examine her child's body for marks of violence, inflammation or venereal disease, sometimes calling in other married women neighbours to give their opinion.[14] A mother's suspicions were also alerted if her child came home with sweets, money or another gift, all signs of dubious adult attention: 'She seemed frightened & I saw that she had been crying. She had two pence and some chocolate in her pocket which I am sure she did not take out with her'.[15] The adage 'don't take sweets from strangers' seems to have been an old one.

The next step, so the depositions reveal, was to take the child to a doctor for confirmation, or directly to the police station to press a charge. Frequently, too, parents would go round to the abuser's house, either with or without a policeman, to confront him about the matter. It was in these latter stages that fathers were more likely to be involved. In this 1875 case the father went round to confront the accused, returning later with a police officer:

> I told him what the child had said, that he'd been taking liberties with my child on two or three occasions. He strongly denied it, & said he never did such a thing in his life ... he said his wife had better come round and see my wife ... I went on Monday morning in consequence of what the child had said & took her with me to his room before him and his wife ... I ... told the child to tell her own story before him & his wife & to tell the truth & nothing but the truth – and the child explained everything that occurred before him & his wife & the Sergeant.[16]

These adult witnesses tell a story of recourse to the police as an obvious and fairly immediate means of dealing with the situation.

Robert Storch has demonstrated there was a high level of conflict between communities and police in northern England during the nineteenth century, and has argued that the police were another official arm intending to impose middle-class moral judgements on the poor.[17] Undoubtedly many Londoners would have agreed with Kathleen Woodward's comment in *Jipping Street*, set in turn-of-the-century Peckham, that: 'I had been brought up with a healthy dislike of policemen.'[18] There were undoubtedly areas of London which took on the nature of ghettos, and which outsiders, including the police, were reluctant to enter. 'The Nichol', in London's East End, was a group of streets and alleys which, according to Arthur Harding, 'bore an evil reputation and was regarded by the working-class people of Bethnal Green as so disreputable that they avoided contact with its people'.[19] Attitudes to the police among London's diverse communities were undoubtedly complex, ranging from acceptance to resentment and hostility; there were marked differences of opinion and experience between those who identified themselves as 'respectable' or law-abiding, those who had been involved in industrial disputes, and those who lived in the slums. It would appear, however, that in certain circumstances the police were seen as useful by elements of the labouring and poorer classes, who chose to utilise the law to retain the moral boundaries, values and standards of their communities. The police could be employed as a part of community self-regulation rather than operating simply as a ruling hegemony trying to impose alien standards. The work of Jennifer Davis and Caroline Conley has done much to demonstrate how magistrates and police worked with London neighbourhoods, how the police courts were used to arbitrate the disputes of the London poor, and how the values and priorities of the local community dominated proceedings.[20] Davis, in her study of the factional disputes between residents of Jennings' Buildings, a West London rookery, has shown that 'it was quite possible for individuals who experienced the law as oppressive in certain circumstances, to use it on their own behalf or others";[21] she has argued that working people, from many different backgrounds, used the courts with confidence.

A distinctive feature in the cases of sexual abuse which ended up in court is the adamant way in which charges were pressed. Accusations could even lead to fisticuffs when shocked and angry parents confronted their children's alleged assailants. Mothers, such as Mary Clark who set out to confront the neighbour who had indecently assaulted her eleven-year-old daughter in 1895, were frequently at the forefront of the action:

> I . . . said 'Mr [Williams] I want to speak to you a minute. You have been insulting my little girl.' He said 'I have not'. I then hit him twice and knocked him down I punched him when he was down he ran into the back yard of his house & I ran after him & hit him again he ran in & bolted the back door. I opened the window and went after him & pulled him out. I held him in his back garden & said 'I want you to prove your innocence & what you have done to my little girl'.[22]

Although violence was a possible form of retaliation and kadi-justice, court witnesses refused to see it as a permanent means of solving the dispute. In 1905 an Enfield father went in search of the man who had molested his daughter on a footpath:

> I went out to search for the man accompanied by my daughter . . . My daughter suddenly clung to me and said . . . 'That is the man father'. . . I took him into custody & had walked about ten or

twelve yards with him when he commenced to whimper & cry. He said 'I did it sir, I'll never do it again, give me a good hiding & let me go'. I said 'oh no' & I took him to the station & charged him.[23]

Indecent assault was seen as a violation which, once perpetrated, could never be remedied. The witnesses who appeared in court had taken what they felt to be the only appropriate strategy to protect their children and those of others: to hand the abuser over to police custody.

Incest[24]

Out of a total sample of 211 child victims involved in sexual assault proceedings at the Middlesex Sessions 1870–1914, only 4 per cent were said to have been abused by family members; 38 per cent had allegedly been abused by strangers and 39 per cent by persons, other than family members, who were known to them. Half of these incidents were said to have taken place behind closed doors, and half outside. When cases of abuse in the home were reported, they tended to involve male lodgers rather than blood relatives. The fact that incest cases were unusual in the courts was commented on by the newspapers. In a report of a recent Old Bailey trial, it was noted in *The Times* that: 'this case differed from the ordinary circumstances attendant on such charges, inasmuch as the child was the daughter of the prisoner'.[25] Incest, although stigmatised as the most serious form of sexual abuse, was also the most underreported. The strategies just outlined were more likely to break down in these cases; the event itself was far harder to articulate.

The low number of incest cases coming before the courts must, first, be attributed to a legal situation which prevented wives from giving evidence against their husbands in courts of law until 1889. The National Society for the Prevention of Cruelty to Children (NSPCC) commented that: 'Married mothers may protect their husbands' dogs, but not their husbands' children . . . Marriage-lines are made the safeguard of the male savage.'[26] NSPCC campaigns successfully resulted in the 1889 Prevention of Cruelty to Children Act which at last made the evidence of wives admissible.[27] Children without mothers were of course in an even worse predicament about whom to tell. Depositions show them turning to female neighbours, aunts or grandmothers who took them to the police station to press charges.[28]

Even though mothers could not usually give evidence against their husbands prior to 1889,[29] some of them, nevertheless, played an important role in uncovering abuse and taking the matter to the police. In a case which came before the Central Criminal Court in 1880, a Lambeth mother who suspected her husband was brutally assaulting their seven-year-old daughter brought in her landlady and other female friends to help spy on her husband's activities. She pretended to go out to work, but stood in wait with the other women ready to catch her husband in the act; although she herself did not give evidence, her friends did.[30] In an 1885 deposition a detective sergeant of the City police described what happened when he arrested a Clerkenwell man, at his brother-in-law's house, for an alleged assault on his thirteen-year-old daughter:

> I told him he would be charged with a criminal assault upon his daughter. He turned to Mr [Parker] and said 'George do you prefer this charge, for God's sake. Consider what you are doing, think of the exposure of our family.' I said 'It is not your brother-in-law, it is your wife and daughter who prefer the charge.' . . . On the charge being entered in the presence of his wife and daughter, the prisoner turned to his wife and asked her 'Do you mean to do what you say, think of it, don't go any further. I will go away and never trouble you again.'[31]

Once again, the man's wife, although not permitted to give evidence in the court, had been involved in pressing charges. This case demonstrates many of the complexities of reporting incest – disgrace on the family, attempted coercion by husbands, the offering of differing interpretations of family loyalty and duty – complexities which, once again, meant it was less likely to end in the courts.

Other women, in contrast, seem to have acted in protection of their husbands, choosing to do so even after the law on married women witnesses had changed. In one 1890 case it was reported that: 'The wife was called in, but said she would rather not give evidence against her husband.'[32] It was easy to stereotype an unknown stranger in line with the melodramatic tradition of evil and bestiality. When the abuser came from within the family itself, was known as a husband and father, boundaries and guide-lines were no longer clear-cut. Women found it much easier to name strangers as villains than to name their own husbands. When, for example, a Clerkenwell man was seen by witnesses in the act of raping his seven-year-old stepdaughter, 'the mother of the child said she did not want him locked up as she was sure that this would be a warning to him, and he would not do the like again'.[33] We cannot merely assume that she believed the rape of her daughter to be insignificant. For this wife and mother, melo-drama did not provide the right language to describe or imagine either the history or the future of her family. She chose not to label her husband as a beast or villain who should be locked up. Perhaps he was still acting coercively; perhaps her loyalties were torn. The family was probably dependent on the man's wage as a breadwinner and would not have survived if he was imprisoned. Although he might be an abuser, he also had an important family function in terms of bringing money into the house. However heinous his crime, the family relationship was too complex, too ambiguous, to enable this woman to resort to purely melodra-matic description.

While cases of incest were far less likely to end in the courts, neighbourhoods, nevertheless, developed other strategies of condemnation. As a result of oral-history interviews with Birmingham residents who had grown up in the slums in the period 1910–39, Carl Chinn has suggested that gossip, ostraci-sation or 'a bloody good hiding' was the treatment meted out against men who offended the 'moral sensibility' of the commu-nity in this way.[34] A close reading of the minutes of evidence collected for the 1885 Royal Commission on the Housing of the Working Classes suggests that many witnesses told very differ-ent stories from those that appeared summarised in the final report which emphasised the evidence of Lord Shaftesbury and Andrew Mearns and which claimed that moral degradation was widespread. London School Board officials said there was no evidence that bad housing was more likely to lead to incest and, furthermore, that any man who was known to have committed incest was likely to be treated 'with horror amongst the poorest classes'.[35] T. Marchant Williams, an inspector of schools who had visited homes in the Finsbury and Marylebone areas, commented:

I found that when a case of that kind [incest] came to the knowledge even of the lowest people there was an outcry in the neighbourhood. For instance, in the case of a father having intercourse with his child it was known all over the district ... several cases same under my observation where fathers had committed such a crime, and they were marked men in the district, however poor the district was.[36]

The phrase 'marked men' contains within it the strategies of ostracisation and community punishment which were exercised in Birmingham. While these strategies may also have been exercised as a way of dealing with non-familial abusers, they provided a key method for condemning incest, which acknowledged the sensitivity of the family situation, without turning to the courts.

Incest and family structure

The work of Joanna Bourke, Carl Chinn, James Hammerton, Elizabeth Roberts, Ellen Ross and Wally Seccombe has proved invaluable in examining the economic and social bases of marriage, sexual attitudes and reproductive practices which were in operation in working-class communities at the turn of the century.[37] Comparatively few studies, however, have centred on the nature of parent–child relations and the power structures of authority and influence which operated with regard to age. Histories of the child-welfare movement have, by concentrating on the increase in state and philanthropic intervention by the turn of the century, created an exaggerated picture of the policing of working-class families by middle-class social workers.[38] Surely the majority of working-class families were, in effect, outside of this disciplinary gaze? The family must still be considered, to a large extent, as a private patriarchal domain which was more likely to receive censure from next-door neighbours than from middle-class do-gooders.

An examination of incest cases, in which the father–daughter relationship is held to be central, can be used to shed extra light on the position of men as fathers in working-class households and on the nature of their authority over their children, illuminating some of the complex issues connected with changing views of masculinity and male authority in late nineteenth-century society.

It was the authority associated with fatherhood which made

incest a possibility and, in certain situations, a reality. The notion that a wife was the sexual property of her husband was enshrined in law in the legitimation of rape in marriage. The legal situation constructed 'conjugal rights' as an act performed by husbands to which wives must submit. Its effects were felt in the letters written by members of the Women's Co-operative Guild in 1914; as one woman wrote: 'No amount of State help can help the sufferings of mothers until men are taught many things in regard to the right use of the organs of reproduction, and until he realises that the wife's body belongs to herself.'[39]

In her study of motherhood in London, Ross has concluded that sexual intercourse in working-class households was 'something that "belonged" to men and from which women defended themselves'.[40] Hammerton has, similarly, demonstrated that, despite the middle-class idealisation of the companionate marriage, wife-beating was 'mostly taken for granted in many working-class communities'.[41] The position of children in relation to sexual assault in the family was more complex. Incest was seen as a sin in the eyes of the Church but was not actually a criminal offence in England until the 1908 Incest Act outlawed sexual intercourse between blood relations (this did not include stepfathers and stepchildren). Before this, sexual acts involving parents and children could only be prosecuted under age-of-consent legislation. This meant that it was legal in 1880 for a father to have a sexual relationship with his thirteen-year-old-daughter if he could prove that she consented; after the 1885 Criminal Law Amendment Act she had to be over sixteen before it was licit.[42]

Acknowledgement of male authority did not mean that incest was tolerated in working-class neighbourhoods; indeed, as I have shown, it was often greeted with community action and censure. Cases of father–daughter incest which came before the London courts reveal a clear conflict in the minds of defendants: between the rights associated with parental authority and, on the other hand, the shamefulness associated with abuse. The depositions show that men who abused their children did so behind closed doors, and that, although they tried to use the authority associated with fatherhood to get what they wanted from their children, they built up a conspiracy of secrecy to cover their activities and, in particular, to conceal the matter from their wives.

Although the family of Robert Smith, did, indeed, live in one room (the system described as immoral by Lord Shaftesbury), he waited for opportunities when his wife was out, leaving him in charge of the baby and the younger children, to molest seven-year-old Flora. The task was made easier because he worked a shift system and was often at home during the day when his wife was herself out at work. He attempted to use a system of vicious threats in order to keep the child from talking. He had, however, failed to allow for the fact that the parlour in which they lived was separated from the rest of the downstairs rooms by a flimsy partition, which meant every noise was audible. The landlady and other lodgers were amongst those who testified at the Old Bailey as to the dialogue, screaming and crying which indicated to them that he was repeatedly assaulting the child:

> I heard him question [Flora] where her mother was, and she said 'She is gone out'. He said she'd better stop out – then I could hear the tea things rattle as if he were getting his breakfast – Then I heard him say 'Come to me [Flora]'. Then he said 'Did you tell your mother what I done to you the other day?' I did not hear the child say anything. Then he said 'If you do, I'll kill you'.[43]

In court Smith denied the charges against him and claimed that substantial injuries had been inflicted on the child by his wife and other parties 'towards spite to me'.[44] A police officer reported the man's immediate comments on arrest: 'this is the second time they've had me for the same thing. Once at Warwick they took me in but they would not take the charge'.[45] It is probable that the man's confidence in abusing without punishment had encouraged him to continue his assaults on Flora. On this occasion, however, he was not so lucky: the medical evidence was incontrovertible and he was convicted and sentenced to twenty years' penal servitude.

More subtle demonstrations of parental power, such as the offering of favours and bribes, were sometimes used by fathers. In July 1885, thirty-seven-year-old John Thurlow seems to have admitted he had been having a sexual relationship with his thirteen-year-old daughter, Lily, for the period of more than a month but argued that she had consented to everything which had taken place.[46] During committal proceeding at Clerkenwell police court Lily was cross-examined at length, defence counsel suggesting it

had been agreed that she could move schools if she submitted to
his demands, that he had given her sweets and money, and that
visits to her grandmother were subject to her consent to sexual
advances. It was suggested that she had had previous sexual experiences with a male cousin and used to 'do something to herself'
when she was a child, hence implying that her moral reputation
was dubious.[47] Lily denied these allegations and claimed she had
never made any sort of agreement:

> I maintain I have never given my consent – I have been afraid to
> move and speak when he has done it because of his threats. One day
> he showed me a doll in a shop in Seven Sisters road and asked me if
> I would like to have it and I said 'Yes' and he said I should have it
> upon conditions. He did not buy the doll then and when we got
> home and I went to bed he asked me if I would do it, and I said 'No
> if that is the conditions I wait'.[48]

Thurlow's case clearly demonstrates a father's attempts to exert
complex methods of control, based on physical, material and
emotional bribes, in order to initiate and maintain a sexual relationship with his daughter. He attempted to assert his role as
decision-maker regarding Lily's schooling as well as his control
over her relationships with other family members (in this case
access to her grandmother). Lily's version of the story suggests
that these attempts at bribery, when refused, resulted in threats
and incidents of violence. Once again, the abuse always took
place when her mother was out and there was no one else in the
house. Lily was not, however, prepared to remain a victim, and
found a way of speaking to her mother. She told the court that the
matter finally came to light when 'I wrote a note to my mother
and put it under her pillow – and she spoke to me on that subject
the next morning'.[49] The Grand Jury, however, decided there was
not enough evidence to convict (a doctor who examined the girl's
body ten days later could find no sign of violence) and the bill of
indictment was thrown out before it reached the Middlesex
Sessions.

Case studies, therefore, demonstrate the full range of coercive
strategies used by abusive fathers. When the authority and influence associated with the position of father failed to ensure
obedience to demands and requests, defendants fell back on physical and economic demonstrations of power in the form of bribes

and threats. If all else failed then violence might become the final recourse. In 1880 a fifty-four-year-old gardener, John Cummings, was tried at the Old Bailey for the rape of his fifteen-year-old daughter, Maria, who told the court:

> The prisoner came in and said if I would let him do what he wanted, I should never want for anything. I said 'no Father'. He then shut the door and took hold of me and threw me down upon the floor, I tried to get away and screamed and he said he would kill me if I did not hold my noise. [The] Prisoner took out his knife but did not open it.[50]

At the trial the defence attempted to shift the blame by arguing 'that the girl was a consenting party' since she was over thirteen.[51] The jury convicted Cummings and Justice Bowen sentenced him to twenty years' penal servitude.

Several defendants in incest cases attempted suicide, presumably fearful of either the prospect of prison or public shame and humiliation. Cummings attempted to throw himself in front of a railway train when he was with a police escort following arrest.[52] Thurlow also attempted to hang himself in the cell at Tottenham police station on the morning of the committal proceedings.[53] Another defendant, a Battersea painter, filled with remorse when his twelve-year-old daughter died in childbirth following his rape, told the magistrate at South Western police court in 1895: 'I have no wish to escape the consequences of what I have done. I could not look my mates in the face again. I shall never want to come out of prison again.'[54] In 1905 a man convicted of indecently assaulting little girls in a field wrote to the Lord High Justice pleading for mercy for the sake of his wife and family; he spoke of 'disgrace on my boddy a shame to look my famley in the face again'.[55] Thus men who found themselves in court were filled with utter shame, demonstrating their awareness of the condemnation of incest – as an abuse of parental authority – in society. They had not, of course, been too ashamed to commit the offences in the first place, nor to attempt to assert their parental authority to silence and subjugate their children.

There is evidence that, in certain situations, incest was linked with other forms of violence and family conflict: 'It appeared that the prisoner had a quarrel with his wife and struck her when she left the room, leaving her daughter with her husband. She had scarcely gone when the prisoner told his daughter to lie down on the bed. She refused and he then took hold of her.'[56] Many of the cases of incest in the London case sample, while not referring directly to husband–wife violence, do nevertheless indicate there was conflict between mother and father, although it is not always clear whether this conflict arose prior to or as a result of the discovery of the father's abuse.

Ross has suggested that, in London at the end of the century, interpersonal tensions which resulted from seasonal and short-term employment patterns could erupt into domestic violence at home. The man's notional authority as head of the family, which had come to be associated with his position as 'breadwinner', was challenged in a labour market where unemployment and lack of security were the order of the day.[57] The sense of powerlessness in the public sphere of work meant that, on the one hand, male authority was eroded within the household and, on the other, individual men might feel a greater need to reassert and empha-sise their authority in the private sphere. In his work on violence in middle-class families, Hammerton has reached comparable conclusions: that men who felt that their authority was threat-ened, perhaps as a result of the spread of more 'chivalric' ideals of masculine behaviour, might turn to violence against wives and children.[58]

It is also important to consider the wider male assumption that every woman had her price; that sex was a commodity which could be secured by buying a woman's services. Defendants accused of indecently assaulting girls, whether strangers or neigh-bours, sometimes attempted to 'buy them off' by offering sums of money to the girls or their parents. The defendants Thurlow and Cummings seemed to have assumed that, once their daughters reached the age of consent, they were legitimate sexual targets whose favours could be bought and bargained for. They attempted to use their close proximity to their daughters, spatially, physically and emotionally, as well as the immense amount of control they had over them as fathers to get what they wanted.

The notion of authority under threat does not explain incest itself, but it does explain how incest could quickly become violent. Notions of masculinity which privileged the father over wife and children created an important structure of power, resting on a notion of paternal authority and subservient obedience which could all too easily be abused by Victorian fathers. This is not to set women and children up as victims of their menfolk. Indeed the quarrels between husband and wife demonstrate that male authority was regularly challenged and that it certainly was not assumed to be absolute. The resistance of fifteen-year-old Maria Cummings, who tried to fight off her father until he pulled a knife on her is a similar testimony.[59] What is clear is that the men involved in incest charges expected to have authority over their families and that they became angry when attempts were made to deny this authority; furthermore, they claimed authority as parents to make certain demands, including sexual ones, of their children.

Notes

I would like to thank Meg Arnot, Peter King, John Seed, Carolyn Steedman and Deborah Thom for their valuable comments on material related to this chapter. The names of all victims, defendants and witnesses have been changed in order to preserve anonymity.

1   London Metropolitan Archive, London. Middlesex Sessions Depositions, MJ/SPE/1870/15, no. 15.

2   A. Mearns, *The Bitter Cry of Outcast London* (London, Frank Cass, [1883] 1970), p. 10.

3   'Report of the Royal Commission on the Housing of the Working Classes': *Parliamentary Papers*, 1884–85, XXX.1, p. 13.

4   A. Wohl, 'Sex and the Single Room: Incest among the Victorian Working Classes', in A. Wohl (ed.), *The Victorian Family: Structure and Stresses* (London, Croom Helm, 1978).

5   A. Davin, *Growing Up Poor: Home, School and Street in London 1870–1914* (London, Rivers Oram Press, 1996), p. 51. Davin also explains how residents of one-room tenements often constructed screens, made from sheets, to preserve modesty.

6   J. Walkowitz, *City of Dreadful Delight: Narratives of Sexual Danger in Late Victorian London* (London, Virago, 1992), p. 94.

7   N. Davis, *Fiction in the Archives: Pardon Tales and Their Tellers in Sixteenth-Century France* (Oxford, Polity Press, 1987), p. 5.

8   For further details see L. A. Jackson, 'Child Sexual Abuse and the Law: London 1870–1914' (unpublished Ph.D. thesis, University of Surrey, 1997).

9   MJ/SPE/1875/21, no. 9; MJ/SPE/1870/14, no. 26; MJ/SPE/1870/16, no. 21; *Hampstead and Highgate Express*, 20 May 1882, p. 4; MJ/SPE/1880/12, no. 8; MJ/SPE/1880/30, no. 30; MJ/SPE/4 Aug. 1900, no. 21; MJ/SPE/7 May 1910, no. 24.
10   J. T. Irvine, 'Insult and Responsibility: Verbal Abuse in a Wolof Village', in J. H. Hill and J. T. Irvine (eds), *Responsibility and Evidence in Oral Discourse* (Cambridge, Cambridge University Press, 1993).
11   Walkowitz, *City of Dreadful Delight*, pp. 85–6.
12   E. Ross, *Love and Toil: Motherhood in Outcast London 1870–1918* (Oxford, Oxford University Press, 1993), p. 166.
13   MJ/SPE/1875/01, no. 29.
14   See for example MJ/SPE/1875/21, no. 49.
15   MJ/SPE/25 May 1895, no. 8.
16   MJ/SPE/1875/01, no. 29.
17   R. Storch, 'The Policeman as Domestic Missionary: Urban Discipline and Popular Culture in Northern England 1850–1880', *Journal of Social History*, 4 (1970) pp. 481–509.
18   K. Woodward, *Jipping Street* (London, Virago, 1993), p. 87.
19   R. Samuel, *East End Underworld: Chapters in the Life of Arthur Harding* (London, Routledge & Kegan Paul, 1981), p. 2.
20   J. Davis, 'A Poor Man's System of Justice: The London Police Courts in the Second Half of the Nineteenth Century', *Historical Journal*, 27:2 (1984) pp. 309–35; J. Davis, 'Prosecutions and Their Context: The Use of Criminal Law in Later Nineteenth-Century London', in D. Hay and F. Snyder (eds), *Policing and Prosecution in Britain 1750–1880* (Oxford, Clarendon Press, 1989) pp. 397–426; C. A. Conley, *The Unwritten Law: Criminal Justice in Victorian Kent* (Oxford, Oxford University Press, 1991).
21   Davis, 'Prosecutions and Their Context', p. 418.
22   MJ/SPE/6 July 1895, no. 30.
23   MJ/SPE/5 Aug. 1905, no. 9.
24   The 1908 Punishment of Incest Act, 8 Edw. VII, c. 45, viewed incest as sexual intercourse within prohibited degrees of consanguinity. I use the term more widely here to apply not only to blood relations (father–daughter, uncle–niece) but to relations by marriage (step-father–stepdaughter, aunt's husband–aunt's niece) who might form part of either a nuclear or an extended family group.
25   *The Times*, 14 March 1870, p. 11.
26   NSPCC, *Annual Report for 1887* (London, NSPCC, 1887), p. 13.

27 The 1889 Prevention of, and Protection of Cruelty to, Children Act, 52 & 53 Vict., c. 44.

28 See MJ/SPE/1880/30, no. 51.

29 For an exception see MJ/SPE/1875/16, no. 11.

30 Public Record Office, London. Central Criminal Court Depositions, CRIM 1/8/2.

31 MJ/SPE/1885/39, no. 2.

32 *West London Observer*, 7 June 1890, p. 3.

33 *Illustrated Police News*, 30 Oct. 1875, p. 3.

34 C. Chinn, *They worked All Their Lives: Women of the Urban Poor in England 1880–1939* (Manchester, Manchester University Press, 1988), p. 42.

35 'Minutes of Evidence of the Royal Commission on the Housing of the Working Classes', *Parliamentary Papers*, 1884–85, XXX.1, Q. 5873, Mr T. Marchant Williams; see also Q. 1525, Mr J. F. Aysh, London School Board visitor.

36 *Ibid.*, Qs. 5872–5, Mr T. Marchant Williams.

37 J. Bourke, 'Housewifery in working-class England 1860–1914', *Past and Present*, 143 (1994) pp. 167–97; Chinn, *They worked All Their Lives*; A. J. Hammerton, *Cruelty and Companionship: Conflict in Nineteenth-Century Married Life* (London, Routledge, 1992); E. Roberts, *A Woman's Place: An Oral History of Working-Class Women 1890–1940* (Oxford, Blackwell, 1986); Ross, *Love and Toil*; W. Seccombe, 'Starting to Stop: Working-Class Fertility in Britain', *Past and Present*, 126 (1990) pp. 151–88.

38 For example, H. Hendrick, *Child Welfare: England 1872–1989* (London, Routledge, 1994); L. Mahood, *Policing Gender, Class and Family: Britain 1850–1940* (London, UCL Press, 1995); H. Ferguson, 'Cleveland in History: the Abused Child and Child Protection, 1880–1914' in R. Cooter (ed.), *In the Name of the Child. Health and Welfare 1880–1940* (London, Routledge, 1992).

39 M. L. Davies, *Maternity: Letters from Working Women. Collected by the Women's Co-operative Guild* (London, Virago, [1915] 1978), p. 27.

40 Ross, *Love and Toil*, p. 101. See also Chinn, *They worked All Their Lives*, p. 142, and Roberts, *A Woman's Place*, p. 84, for similar findings. Seccombe, 'Starting to Stop', p. 176, has suggested the picture was not quite so bleak and that some men were co–operative and, indeed, supportive of wives who wanted to avoid pregnancy.

41 Hammerton, *Cruelty and Companionship*, p. 19. See also Chinn, *They worked All their Lives*, p. 14.
42 The 1885 Criminal Law Amendment Act, 48 & 49 Vict. c. 69.
43 CRIM 1/8/2.
44 *Ibid.*
45 *Ibid.*
46 *Pall Mall Gazette*, 16 July 1885, p. 10.
47 MJ/SPE/1885/39, no. 21.
48 *Ibid.*
49 *Ibid.*
50 CRIM 1/8/8.
51 *Illustrated Police News*, 5 June 1880, p. 4.
52 *Ibid.*
53 *Pall Mall Gazette*, 16 July 1885, p. 10.
54 *The Times*, 17 July 1895, p. 3.
55 MJ/SPE/30 Sept. 1905, loose papers.
56 *Illustrated Police News*, 2 Oct. 1875, p. 3.
57 Ross, *Love and Toil*, pp. 58, 74.
58 Hammerton, *Cruelty and Companionship*, pp. 149–50.
59 CRIM 1/8/8.

Lost childhoods: recovering children's experiences of welfare in modern Scotland

The investigation of children's subjectivity in the past poses particular problems for the historian. As the history of children and childhood has developed in recent years it has become clear that it is easier to write about children as objects of policy or about the concept of childhood than it is to enter the realm of childhood experience. As Hugh Cunningham remarked, 'those seeking to capture the emotional quality of the lives of children in the past encounter formidable hurdles'.[1] The subordination of experience to the framing of ideas and policies is especially evident in the history of child welfare and protection which has taken little notice of children's views and their responses to policies enacted on their behalf. Perhaps it is time for historians to take on board some of the ideas and methodologies utilised by social-welfare practitioners and child psychologists in an attempt to reach beyond a functional understanding of the impact of welfare policy on those who lived it. Using a range of personal testimony this chapter is an attempt to reclaim the voice of the child (through adult reminiscence) in order to draw attention to the ways in which children dealt with an objectively traumatic situation, that is, being cared for outwith their natural family.

The focus here is Scotland after the First World War where a combination of severe social dislocation in the cities and poverty in the rural Lowlands and Highlands meant the family was uniquely unstable and where children, the most vulnerable victims of family breakdown, were treated as guinea pigs in a progressive long-term experiment carried out by a matrix of child-welfare practitioners, voluntary organisations and religious charities. The damaging consequences of some aspects of child-care involving physical mistreatment, cruelty and abuse are only now coming to light in Scotland as elsewhere, but the broader picture of a range of care solutions, dominated by foster care and supplemented by a network of institutions, suggests a rather more ambiguous legacy from the point of view of those who spent their childhood years being cared for outwith their natural family.

In the decade before 1914, between 70,000 and 80,000 orphaned, neglected and destitute children were found homes by the English authorities every year, the majority – at least until the turn of the century – maintained in residential care. Another 10,000 Scottish children needed homes after being orphaned, left destitute or cruelly treated or having become an impossible burden for a lone parent, but unlike in England the Scottish authorities – the Poor Law boards and subsequently local government departments – eschewed residential care, preferring to board out homeless children with relatives or strangers. In 1914 more than 80 per cent of children in the care of the Poor Law authorities were placed with foster families. This is not to say that residential care was not a feature of the Scottish child welfare system. Indeed, two of the largest children's homes in the British Isles were located north of the border: the Orphan Homes of Scotland, popularly known as William Quarrier's Homes, at Bridge of Weir near Glasgow, which had a peak capacity of up to 1,000, and Aberlour Orphanage on Speyside in the north-east which cared for more than 2,000 children between 1875 and 1914. In addition most size-able towns had at least one residential childcare institution usually run by a religious order or a philanthropic individual motivated by a sense of evangelical mission. However, residential care was undoubtedly regarded as the poor relation of the boarding-out system in Scotland; a policy which was continually reaffirmed from the early nineteenth century through to the 1960s. In 1864 the Glasgow City Children's Committee expressed the opinion that:

> [boarded-out children] do not certainly come in from school or play with the precise, demure and well-disciplined appearance that you find in a well-managed orphanage, but what pleases the committee more, they appear with a buoyancy of spirit, a confidence of manner, and happiness of countenance.[2]

The confidence in the boarding-out system expressed by the Glasgow authorities was echoed a few years later by the Poor Law Inspector J. J. Henley who, in a report to the English Poor Law Board, praised the benefits of foster care. 'We believe that children brought up in public institutions, when at length turned out in the world, are, as a general rule, feeble in body and mind, and less able to fight their way through life than those who come from the common walks of society.' He continued, 'At present our children are living amidst, and already form part of the labouring community in which their after life is to be spent.'[3] Institutional care, it was believed, perpetuated hereditary pauperism. Any sense of self-reliance was destroyed in the disciplinary atmosphere of the poor house. Scottish boarded-out children were favourably compared with their English counterparts who, it was said, 'spoke in half whispers and lacked the spontaneity of youth'.[4] In the light of these convictions Scotland's pauper children were mostly found new homes with strangers throughout the rural parts of the country, from the southern Lowlands to the much favoured Highlands and Islands. The city parishes of Glasgow, Edinburgh and Aberdeen were enthusiastic advocates of rural foster care. By 1895 Glasgow's inner-city Barony parish had children boarded from Dumfries in the south to Tomintoul and Buckie in the northeast and on the islands of Islay and Iona. Crofting society was regarded as a natural and healthy environment for urban slum children. Following a visit to the Island of Arran, a favourite location for pauper children until the Island's owner, the Duke of Hamilton, objected to what he regarded as the creation of 'pauper villages', the Board of Supervision inspector enthused about the relative advantages of the island environment for deprived, sickly urban children:

> To find the younger children . . . after school hours, enjoying themselves on the sea beach, playing about the family hearth, running messages for the family to the nearest shop . . . or looking after the cows, or sheep, or poultry, helping to plant potatoes, or engaged in any of the many rural avocations of crofters' children – amidst beautiful scenery, and in a healthy climate, with good lodging, wholesome food, and decent and sufficient clothing – is so great a contrast to the life of the children in the lanes and bye-streets of the great towns, or even in the well-regulated Poorhouses.[5]

The preference for boarding out over residential care continued to characterise Scottish child welfare through the interwar years. Indeed, in 1933, a peak year for homeless children, more than 8,000 children out of a total of 9,200 were found foster homes, the majority with strangers who were paid an allowance for taking these children into their homes.[6] And in 1946 the report of the government's committee of inquiry into the provision of care for homeless children in Scotland (the Clyde Committee), while recommending more stringent selection of foster parents and the abandonment of boarding out city children in remote areas, once again reaffirmed the Scottish commitment to foster care concluding that 'a good foster parent system should be encouraged as the best solution of the problem, as it is most suited to give the child the necessary individual attention, and scope for the development of its independence and initiative'.[7] As a result, boarding out remained the favoured solution for homeless children in local-authority care until the 1960s and Glasgow continued to find distant rural homes, including on the islands of the Inner and Outer Hebrides, for its children until a policy change in the 1970s. Residential care was a short-term and temporary solution for children in local-authority care although for individuals in distress the local children's home was often the first port of call.

The Clyde Committee addressed both the material and emotional care of children. Their investigations and report reveal a greater awareness of the strong bonds between children and their birth parents which had been highlighted by a number of studies of children evacuated during the Second World War.[8] Simultaneously, concern about the emotional and psychological welfare of such children was being addressed by educational psychologists and psychiatrists and those involved in the Child Guidance movement. In the early days those responsible for the welfare of homeless children were primarily concerned with physical health and only tangentially engaged with issues of psychological and emotional disturbance by trying to ensure children boarded out or placed in a children's home could not be distinguished by means of a uniform or separate treatment and by denying them information about their birth families and background. By the post Second World War era, however, it was recognised by childcare professionals that many homeless children were emotionally disturbed and traumatised by their pre-care experiences which in turn affected their general behaviour and their educational development. As the headmaster of the Orphan Homes of Scotland (Quarrier's) School, C. H. Galletly, pointed out, by the 1940s a large proportion of children placed in children's homes and boarded out were not the homeless and destitute of the nineteenth century but so-called 'problem' children 'who need, above all else, expert understanding and psychological help'.[9] When asked whether there was a large proportion of problem children in the home, Mr Galletly replied, '850'; this was the total number of children cared for by Quarrier's Homes.[10] In spite of this no psychiatrist had ever been appointed to a post at the Orphan Homes although Child Guidance had been pioneered in Glasgow, the first Child Guidance Clinic being established there in 1931 bringing together the expertise of a psychiatrist, psychologist and psychiatric social worker.[11] In spite of the lack of psychiatric support at Quarrier's Homes, however, the Clyde Committee was alerted to the need for a child welfare service that was more sensitive to the individual needs of the children it served. In his evidence to the Committee in 1945 an expert on child psychiatry stated:

> All previous studies and investigations have shown that it is a relatively simple matter to provide shelter, warmth and nourishment, but that it is difficult to reproduce those conditions which will satisfy the child's needs for affection and discipline, security and happiness, so naturally provided by the family and without which the child has little chance of developing in a healthy and normal manner. Nothing can ever compensate a child for the loss of the care which his own parents can give, but much can be done to give him conditions under which he can develop satisfactorily.[12]

Indeed, this witness recommended that every child who was placed under the care of the authorities should be examined by a medical doctor and a psychoanalyst before being boarded out or placed in an institution and this was reiterated in the *Report* of the Clyde Committee published in 1946.[13] The 1948 Children Act reflected this new ethos by placing the duty on local authorities to 'further [the child's] best interests, and to afford him opportunity for the proper development of his character and abilities'.

Since the 1950s, influenced by the work of Freud, the writings of John Bowlby and others on the effects of maternal deprivation on a child's psychopathology have informed both policy towards children in care and our understanding of the child's experience of that care.[14] Bowlby argued that the loss of maternal care in the early years of childhood would have profound consequences for that child's subsequent personality development. In Bowlby's words, 'A break in the continuity of the mother–child relationship at a critical stage in the development of the child's social responses may result in more or less permanent impairment of the ability to make relationships.'[15] On the other hand, follow-up studies demonstrated that mitigating factors could alleviate such psychopathological problems and that the situation which gave rise to the child's separation from the family is just as likely to be a crucial factor in determining subsequent development. In the light of these developments, childcare policy was thoroughly reviewed with the result that most of the large orphanages were closed, to be replaced by smaller homes, and the boarding out of children far away from their families was abandoned in Scotland. In 1992 there were only 4,840 children in Scotland being cared for outwith their natural families – the majority in foster care – although another 7,242 were living at home under the supervision of local authorities.[16]

Clearly then, by the 1940s, there was a significant degree of official disquiet about the quality and effects of residential and foster care on Scotland's most vulnerable children. At least one serious case of child abuse of two boys boarded out in Fife in 1945 claimed public attention and forced the authorities in Scotland to take a close look at their childcare system which, until then, had been favourably compared with policy south of the border.[17] In addition child-welfare professionals were, by then, armed with a mass of evidence which pointed to mistreatment, physical and mental abuse, emotional neglect, exploitation and educational underachievement gleaned from official inspectors, questionnaires, and verbal and written evidence presented to committees by adults in positions of authority. However, there was never any sustained or serious attempt to elicit the views of the children themselves. By accessing retrospective accounts of childhoods spent in institutions or foster care between the First World War and the 1960s this chapter aims to provide a more nuanced and child-centred understanding of the impact of the distinctive Scottish child welfare system.[18] The consequence is a fresh analysis of the impact of boarding out and residential care on children which suggests that the structure of care is far less significant than has been believed hitherto.

Recent revelations of the extent of abuse of children in residential care throughout the British Isles have reinforced a long-standing mistrust of childcare institutions.[19] Allegations that a number of children's homes in England, Wales and Scotland meted out brutal and sadistic treatment to vulnerable children have served to bolster the popular view – in Scotland and more widely – that foster care is a more enlightened and sympathetic means of caring for homeless children. Yet, official and popular beliefs in the benefits of boarding out compared with the disadvantages of residential care are not necessarily borne out by the experiences of individual children. Although it would be invidious and unhelpful to attempt to compare the experiences of the two sets of children – there were good and bad experiences of both forms of care – nevertheless personal reminiscences do illustrate the complexity and ambiguity of childhood experience and furthermore indicate the points of comparison rather than difference between the two systems.

At first sight personal reminiscences would appear to support the policy preference for boarding out over residential care. Despite the attempts of some orphanage directors – William Quarrier especially – to recreate a family atmosphere along the lines of Barnardo's cottage-style home at Barkingside, orphanage children recall the discipline, the regimentation, the lack of freedom and spontaneity, and the impersonal nature of institutional life, indeed all those aspects of residential care so abhorred by nineteenth-century policy-makers. 'Aberlour Orphanage aims at being a Home, not an institution and it succeeds in that ambition' was the proud claim of the warden of that large institution in 1925. 'Visitors frequently remark that the children do not look in the least like Institution children. They wear no uniform, are not hampered by unnecessary and unnatural rules, and run about the place as freely as if they were in their own homes.'[20] Such claims bore little relationship to some children's experience. 'It was a strict, uniformed, episcopalian upbringing', recalled one former Aberlour resident, 'where cleanliness, discipline and religion were adhered to'.[21] Scotland's principal Roman Catholic children's home, Smyllum Orphanage at Lanark, was described by inspectors in 1945 as 'terribly inhuman'. 'There was a subnormal look about [the children] and they seemed oppressed.'[22] Annie, who spent seven years from the age of seven in a small Aberdeen home run by a female religious order, recalled:

[I]t wasn't a life when you look back ... I just made the best of it, I made the best of it ... But on the whole I wouldn't say I was unhappy, because we didn't know what it was to be happy, you see ... it was just an existence from morning to night.[23]

The pervasiveness of the disciplinary regime in some institutions is clear in the memories of former residents who recall in detail the daily routine, the predictable menu, the suppression of children's natural exuberance. Annie recalled being 'frightened to do anything wrong ... The religion wouldn't let us do that.'[24] 'We rarely "played" as normal children do', wrote another woman sent to a 'very famous Scottish orphanage'; 'we had no time to play because *all* domestic duties were done by us'.[25] The stifling regimes operated by a number of the larger homes in particular did not go unnoticed. One expert witness called to give evidence to the 1945 Clyde Committee was outspoken in his criticism of the disciplinary regimes which appeared to benefit only those charged with the children's care:

One of the great difficulties is that these big homes are unnatural. They are too clean, too orderly, and too quiet. Naturally the supervisors want orderliness and cleanliness and quietness, but sometimes it is absolutely pathetic. You see groups of boys playing football and never a sound. You see large rooms of toddlers 'playing' and never a sound. Everything is polished to the highest degree. Everything is clean and neat and tidy. No wonder the poor kiddies get complexes.[26]

Implicit in the disciplinary regime was the cultivation of a rather impersonal environment which hindered individuality. Upon admission to an institution children were divested of their personal belongings and dressed in orphanage attire. Annie vividly recalled the outfit she wore upon arrival with her sister at the age of seven at Aberdeen's Bethany Home. 'It was a blue costume, pleated skirts, I think I see it yet ... a double breasted jacket with brass buttons, and a black velour hat, black stockings and shoes.'[27] This smart and clearly much loved outfit was replaced with a dress and pinafore with skirts so long the girls used to hitch them up once they got to school and ill-fitting boys' boots with eyelets which she picked out 'because I didnae like them'.[28] Boys at Aberlour Orphanage were given a distinctive short haircut: 'you did get a crop', recalled Arthur, 'you were known . . . If you ran away they would pick you up.'[29] Moreover, right up until the 1960s boys were also dressed in kilts for Sundays and outings. 'Thinking back now', said one former resident,

> people must have looked at us going about in our kilts, thinking what's this? . . . you used to get people, tourists used to stop and take a photo of you for some reason . . . Yes you sort of stood out from the crowd, you had short hair and people did look at you, you did feel a bit different . . . I used to hate the kilt . . . the times of the Beatles and that sort of thing.[30]

Despite official reservations about placing children in an institutional environment since the early nineteenth century, it was not until the 1940s that such disquiet was publicly addressed and debated following the lessons learned of children's experiences of evacuation and residential care during the Second World War. Earlier fears of orphanage children lacking independence and spirit were superseded by concerns about interpersonal relationships. Long-term residential care, it was believed, had a deleterious affect on children's ability to form sound relationships with others. Such children were observed to develop a 'curious sense of detachment' which inhibited their ability to make friends.[31] Dorothy Burlingham and Anna Freud in their influential study of children cared for in residential nurseries during the war discovered that older children's relationships with one another were characterised by aggression, indifference and jealousy.[32] Individuals' memories of care support these findings. Amongst boys especially, the loneliness and sense of isolation are striking. 'I thought I lived in Aberlour with crowds', reflected Arthur, adding, 'there was only one or two people I would speak to and confide in'. Having been separated from his four siblings, he 'felt very lonely being separated from the rest of the family and I felt myself wanting to be with them'.[33] David, who was admitted to Aberlour with his four brothers and sisters recalled that he 'never really thought about my brothers and sisters, there was just me and that was it'. 'I was in my own little world anyway'.[34] Another Aberlour resident noted, 'To the observer there may have appeared to be a sense of order and discipline, even calm and contentment, about the orphanage. But to me it was a world I felt apart from, did not belong to, and which I felt unable to come to terms with.'[35]

There are few indications that boys shared personal feelings with other boys, preferring to adopt psychological defences against a repressive and sometimes violent regime. 'You did fight a lot actually, there were quite a few fights and you had to look after yourself, any sign of weakness and you got a bit of abuse', recalled David.[36] Girls, on the other hand, do appear to have formed friendships or support networks in order to deal with their sense of isolation. Christine's memories of Aberlour in the 1930s mirror other contemporaneous accounts celebrating female friendships:

> I suppose you're unhappy ... but you just don't remember very much about it because there's so many of you together and you're all telling each other your sad stories you know ... and if somebody was crying we'd say 'what's wrong?', 'I'm thinking of my Mum', so we'd give her all our toys and then the next day it'd be her turn to give them all back to somebody else.[37]

And yet the bullying and isolation of a child who was different in some way was one of the consequences of the abnormal relationships formed in the residential care environment. One former resident of Aberlour later reflected upon the cruelty children could mete out to others:

> There were the unfortunate ones who mentally or educationally were not quite up to the mark; the children who were always behind, dragging along with all sorts of handicaps which at that time had to be endured rather than alleviated. At first these children had shocked me. I was sorry for them, but I didn't want to associate with them. I kept myself aloof from the bed-wetters forever washing and drying their soiled sheets, and the girls whose heads were shaven because of ringworm. Suppose I were to catch it and have my head shaved?[38]

Unlike most children, those in residential care had no means of escape from a bullying situation. Dorothy spent a profoundly

unhappy time in care being victimised by other girls and members
of staff who locked her in cupboards, tied her to the bed and
pulled her hair 'from one end of the road to another'.[39] Her older
brothers and sisters were unable to protect her and her experience
in care had a profound long-term impact.

In 1946 a former resident and housemaster at Aberlour
Orphanage expressed the opinion that this institution 'could
never fill the place of a normal home with the intimate family life
cycle, in the life of a child'. He continued:

> The Orphanage, despite its proud boast of providing a 'homely'
> home for children in the first place is structurally unable to live up
> to its boast ... When a boy is admitted to the orphanage he ceases
> to be an individual, his personality is submerged ... In a short time
> he has become as mediocre, listless and apathetic as the other boys
> in the house ... Through time he becomes used to the cold imper-
> sonality of the place and becoming so used to it, people mistake it
> for happiness.[40]

Children who spent years in residential care did become institutionalised to some degree. Life amidst a crowd of other children
isolated from the rest of society bred insecurity in some which
affected them in later years. 'Some things are better about the
home', recalled one respondent, 'but you lost a lot in your life
afterwards. Like, you lost your confidence ... and when I came
out I felt a complex ... there's a stain on you, a stain.'[41]
Similarly, David reflected that,

> even to this day, I still react the way I did in the orphanage some-
> times, its never grown out of me, I'm very defensive, very defensive
> ... It was worse when I left the home really (...) because it was
> secure in the orphanage, it was a wee world of your own ... it was
> your only world.[42]

It was for precisely these reasons that Scotland's childcare
authorities had for so long rejected residential care for the majority of its homeless children. Foster care, or boarding out, was the
ideal substitute for a 'normal' family life, a home from home
which would meet the physical *and* emotional needs of children.
'A kindly, warm-hearted guardian is the most important and can
go a long way to make up for what the child has missed', asserted
one submission to the Clyde Committee:

> Life in a home, in a household where a child is taken in as one of
> the family, has an advantage over any institution. It shares the ups
> and downs of family life and learns to give and take, and takes part
> in the pleasures and disappointments of the family. This is a far
> better preparation for life than to live in even a small institution.[43]

The intention of the authorities was to produce healthy, well-
adjusted children who would make their own way in life,
unhindered by their 'degenerate' parents and relatives and free
from the temptations of the city. Even today, few would disagree
with the premise that a child is most likely to thrive in a family
environment as opposed to an institution, and this was certainly
the view of the Curtis Committee in England and Wales which
concluded in 1946 that boarding out was still preferable to institutional care even when there was 'probably greater risk of acute
unhappiness in a foster home', implying that a few unfortunate
victims of unscrupulous or abusive guardians were a price worth
paying for the greater good of the majority who experienced a
happy and supportive foster environment.[44] Two high-profile
cases of severe cruelty to children by guardians in Shropshire and
Fife respectively in 1945, had highlighted the shortcomings of a
boarding-out system which failed to carry out even the most rudimentary checks on potential foster parents but even the death of
one child and appalling cruelty to two others did not have a decisive impact upon official policy which was characterised above all
by complacency.

'How could you expect', remarked an informed critic of
boarding out in 1945, 'children from the slums of our big cities
where they have been accustomed to noise and bustle, crowds
and the ever-changing excitement of the city, to be suddenly
transplanted to the island of Mull, where one sees nothing but
mountains and water, rain and snow, cattle and sheep?'[45]
Surprisingly, many children boarded out to the Highlands and
Islands from inner-city areas did in fact thrive in their new environment and adapted remarkably well. Betty who was boarded
out on the island of Tiree from Glasgow in 1943 commented
that, 'Tiree was one of the lucky places ... it was a good place
for children to be' as the islanders were almost self-sufficient in
foodstuffs. 'Look at the milk, there was gallons of the stuff ...
All there was to do was buy a bag of oatmeal and make

porridge, the potatoes ... a lot of fish ... and they were baking all the time.'[46] And yet placing children in the countryside was no guarantee that they would be protected from harm, social isolation or the stigma of pauperism.

Compared with the physical isolation of children in residential care, boarded-out children appear to have been integrated into the local community and yet popular attitudes towards these children were ambiguous to say the least. While vociferous opposition to the removal of city children to Highland and Island communities had ceased by the turn of the century, the majority of respondents remember numerous ways in which they were made to feel different. Despite the insistence of the authorities that boarded-out children should not wear the 'pauper stamp' such children inevitably stood out when dressed in the clothes provided by the Corporation. 'I remember well you'd get long trousers that reached well past your knees' commented one Tiree resident; 'They looked awful those trousers. The other boys in school had neat, short trousers and that was a pointer, you know, that these lads weren't the same as people's own sons.'[47] It was common practice for boarded-out children to use their own surname but often with the foster family's surname in brackets afterwards which caused confusion and misunderstanding at school and especially amongst school friends. 'I found out when I was seven that I didn't belong', said a woman happily boarded out in Aberdeenshire. A friend told her, 'he's not your father in any case, it's not your family'.[48] Former 'boarded-outs' remember name-calling by their schoolfellows and their parents – 'Glasgow orphans', 'Glasgow kealies' and 'homies'. 'Even at school', said Betty, 'they would turn around and say you're just boarded out.'[49] 'Kids will be kids', recalled Robert brought up in the small close-knit fishing village of Buckie on the north-east coast:

> and you used to get the brickbats at school, Glasgow orphan this and that and you were called names and again – it wasnae so bad, it was acceptable to you as a kid ... but again you see if there was any devilment ... the adult parent's 'mine can do no wrong, it's those Glasgow orphans' and that you know that's what you're up against ... there was a differential kind of system there you see.[50]

In Gaelic-speaking communities integration was made even more difficult. The cultural shock of arriving in a place where people spoke another language was graphically described by Bernard Mac a'Ghobhainn:

> When my brother and I came here on the Oban–Tiree ferry we heard people speaking but we didn't understand what they said. We thought they were Germans but they were Tiree people coming back from the sales in Oban. We were a bit worried by this but in fact they were speaking Gaelic.[51]

'I think I knew I was on an island', remarked Betty, 'but I don't think we were told now you're going to this place and don't be surprised if you don't understand what they say.'[52]

However, it was the family environment above all else that was crucial to a child's sense of well-being and belonging. In the early years of boarding out the Glasgow City Children's Committee had expressed the view that 'the family circle is the most natural one for the bringing up and training of children', in which 'these children look upon the heads of the family as their parents, and the younger branches as brothers and sisters.'[53] Guardians were instructed that 'a kindly feeling should be cultivated between the guardians and the children, who ought to be treated, as far as possible, as members of the family in which they are boarded.'[54] Probably the majority of children were well cared for and treated as one of the family. 'I cannot imagine', wrote one man boarded out in Peterhead, 'how anybody could have received more love and attention than I did.'[55] 'I *was* to all intents and purposes their daughter', commented a woman sent by Glasgow Corporation to a village in Aberdeenshire.[56] The affections of many children lay with their foster family, a feeling expressed by one man boarded on Tiree. 'Many think that a mother is the one who gives birth to you', explained Pol MacCaluim. 'But she's not. The one who raises you, that's your mother.'[57]

Yet, the boarding-out system inevitably had its casualties. The reliance on twice or thrice yearly cursory inspection visits and the naive belief that cases of child neglect and abuse would be prevented by community policing left children vulnerable to exploitation and mistreatment. There had always been suspicions on the part of the authorities that some guardians took in children purely for financial gain. The economic reality, at least in crofting communities, meant that children's contributions were often essential for the maintenance of a standard of living and the allowances paid to guardians in addition to the work boarded-out children might undertake could make a substantial difference to the family income. Naomi Mitchison in her capacity as a member of the Clyde Committee in 1945–46 noticed in poor homes in the Inverness area that 'in many of them the only money coming into the house would be that which the children would bring . . . these remote crofts depend almost entirely on primitive labour'.[58] Nevertheless, while children were expected to do some farm duties and were mostly happy to carry them out, there was a fine line between normal expectations and blatant exploitation. Peter, who spent most of his childhood with a foster mother in a village on the Moray Firth coast, explained how he was inadequately fed and deprived of basic comforts and believed her motivation was 'purely money':

> Material gain because not just what they would be getting from Glasgow Corporation they were obviously gaining something from sending us out to the farm to work, I mean we got nothing for it. We had to slave and do what we had to do so I mean she's bound to have got some reward from that . . . I mean there was no love no.[59]

The popular perception of the position of boarded-out children in Scottish communities does not, by and large, recognise the ill-treatment meted out to some. Yet considerable evidence points to some children being treated as second-class citizens, given inferior food, forced to eat separately from the rest of the family and being barred from parts of the house. 'There was two tables set – one in the kitchen and one in the scullery', recalled one woman. 'Ours was in the scullery, theirs was in the kitchen. They had chicken soup, chicken, potatoes, the lot. Ours consisted of the bones of the chicken and the skin of the chicken.'[60] Peter was never permitted in the parlour where his foster parents and their son lived, ate and listened to the radio; 'we were never treated as one of the family no no you knew exactly what you were'.[61]

Children treated in this way were no better prepared than their counterparts in residential care when they eventually left home. In Peter's words:

> I went about with a chip on my shoulder for a long time you know, why should that have happened to me you know, why should I have been beaten from morning until night . . . I'm just an ordinary

human being but er when you came out and seen how other people lived and started mixing with families and made friends and you saw how they lived ... you know it made you feel bitter.[62]

The personal testimonies cited here do, in their very richness and attention to detail, contribute towards a more nuanced and child-centred understanding of the impact of the child welfare system in the past. They also force us to question the certainty behind the continuous preference of the Scottish child-welfare authorities for foster care on the grounds that children cared for within families would turn out better able to 'fight their way through life' than those brought up in the rigid and oppressive environment of the children's home. Certainly both systems of care had their successes but for those children failed by the system boarding out and residential care present too many similarities for us to ignore. Both childcare solutions perpetuated the homeless child's isolation from other children. The larger children's homes were situated in isolated locations and did not encourage mixing with local children so that some residents remained infantilised and institutionalised. Neither did residential care foster healthy relationships amongst children so that some individuals became victims of taunts and bullying and many others adopted a defensive attitude towards other children. Boarded-out children, often in small communities, were also isolated by the reactions of others, stigmatised by the name-calling and the exclusion from the networks of a close-knit community, here vividly described by Robert on the occasion of his search for work:

and they looked after their own you see, now just take me I wanted to get in to serve my time as a joiner I did you know, but Willie was taken before [me] because Willie's Dad was maybe in the shipyards, I didnae have that push, I didnae have that kick your backside into a job, but this is what you're up against and you accept it right enough.[63]

The comparability of the two systems of care is also evident in the disciplinary nature of the care provided. Children in orphanages and with foster parents were commonly expected to undertake a certain amount of unpaid labour and many were subjected to a system involving the strict enforcement of rules and infliction of punitive punishment.

In experiential terms there is little to distinguish the failures of
the two systems of care despite the contrasting structures of that
care. Children who were poorly treated in institutions and within
families speak in similar terms about the absence of family affection and the loss of their childhood. 'I thought it was wonderful
to be in a home with other people', remarked Annie on leaving
her strict children's home.[64] 'I didn't know how much I'd missed
until I had kids of my own', remarked another woman whose
foster-care experience was unhappy.

> Then I noticed the affection you should get back from children. Wee
> cuddles, wee kisses, things you're supposed to do with them.
> Ordinary living that other people take as everyday, we didn't get.[65]

'I lost my childhood', remarked Donald, 'I had no childhood at
all.'[66]

Notes

1   H. Cunningham, *Children and Childhood in Western Society since
    1500* (London, Longman, 1995), p. 2.
2   Glasgow City Archives (GCA), D-CH 1/1: Children's Committee
    Minute Book, 1852–64, 25 Aug. 1864.
3   J. J. Henley, 'Report on the Boarding out of Pauper Children in
    Scotland, 1870', *Parliamentary Papers*, 1870, LVIII p. 79.
4   Dr Macnamara, Parliamentary Secretary to the Local Government
    Board (1908), cited in H. Hendrick, *Child Welfare: England
    1872–1989* (London, Routledge, 1994), p. 77.
5   W. A. Peterkin, 'Report regarding Pauper Children boarded in the
    Island of Arran by Glasgow and other Parishes', in *Annual Report
    of the Board of Supervision, 1862. Parliamentary Papers*, 1863,
    XXII, Appendix A, no. 4, p. 650.
6   I. Levitt, *Poverty and Welfare in Scotland 1890–1948* (Edinburgh,
    Edinburgh University Press, 1988), p. 209.
7   'Report of the Committee on Homeless Children (Scotland)',
    Parliamentary Papers, 1946 (Cmd 6911), p. 32.
8   See S. Isaacs (ed.), *The Cambridge Evacuation Survey* (London,
    Methuen, 1941); W. Boyd (ed.), *Evacuation in Scotland: A Record
    of Events and Experiments* (Scottish Council for Research in
    Education, London, University of London Press, 1944).
9   Scottish Record Office (SRO), ED 11/161: Committee on Homeless

Children – Evidence of Private Individuals. Personal memorandum from Mr C. H. Galletly, 15 Jan. 1946.

10   SRO, ED 11/266: Committee on Homeless Children – Voluntary Homes etc. Minutes of the Meeting of the Committee on Homeless Children, 30 Jan. 1946. Appendix II, evidence of Mr Galletly.

11   See Olive C. Sampson, *Child Guidance: Its History, Provenance and Future* (Manchester, British Psychological Society, University of Manchester, 1980), p.16.

12   SRO, ED 11/161: Committee on Homeless Children – Evidence of Private Individuals. Memorandum prepared by Dr D. R. Maccalman, 8 Nov. 1945.

13   SRO, ED 11/266: Committee on Homeless Children – Voluntary Homes etc. Minutes of the Meeting of the Committee on Homeless Children, 4 Dec. 1945, Appendix VI.

14   See especially J. Bowlby, *Attachment and Loss*, Vol. II: *Separation* (London, Hogarth Press, 1973).

15   J. Bowlby cited in H. Rudolph Schaffer, *Making Decisions about Children: Psychological Questions and Answers* (Oxford, Blackwell, 1990), p. 118.

16   *Scottish Abstract of Statistics*, vol. XXIV (1995).

17   This was the 'Walton case' involving severe ill-treatment of two brothers by their guardians in Kirkaldy, Fife. *Glasgow Herald*, 23 July 1945.

18   The sources cited are drawn from a number of interviews carried out with former residents of children's homes and those boarded out, as well as correspondence with a number of others. In addition I have used interviews with persons boarded out on the Inner and Outer Hebridean Islands broadcast as *Air Fasdadh* ('Boarded Out') by BBC 2 Scotland and interviews and correspondence with former residents of Aberlour Orphanage generated by a project undertaken by Speyside High School in Aberlour, published as *Childhood Days at Aberlour Orphanage*, with a video of the same title.

19   For example, 'Nuns in Child Cruelty Probe', *Evening Express* (Aberdeen), 10 June 1997; 'Abuse Claims Shake Church', *The Guardian*, 8 Nov. 1997. See also the 1997 tribunal of inquiry into abuse in children's homes in North Wales.

20   *Aberlour Orphanage Jubilee Year* (1925), p. 10.

21   Correspondence with David (all names are fictitious), (born 1951), Aberlour Orphanage, 1955–67.

22   SRO, ED 11/168: Committee on Homeless Children – Report of

Visits to Homes. Visit to Smyllum Orphanage, Lanark, Nov. 1945.

23   Interview with Annie, (born 1907), Bethany House, Aberdeen 1914–21.

24   *Ibid.*

25   SRO, ED 11/154: Committee on Homeless Children. Anonymous letter, 1945.

26   SRO, ED 11/266: Committee on Homeless Children. Evidence of Dr R. D. MacCalman, 1945.

27   Interview with Annie.

28   *Ibid.*

29   Interview with Arthur (born 1911), Aberlour Orphanage, 1920–24.

30   Interview with David (born 1951), Aberlour Orphanage 1955–67.

31   SRO, ED 11/161: Committee on Homeless Children. Evidence of Lilian Russell, Organising Secretary, Moral Welfare Work, the Episcopal Church in Scotland, 16 Nov. 1945.

32   D. Burlingham and A. Freud, *Infants without Families: The Case For and Against Residential Nurseries* (London, Allen & Unwin, 1944).

33   Interview with Arthur.

34   Interview with David.

35   Letter from Ernest (Aberlour Orphanage, 1960s).

36   Interview with David.

37   Interview with Christine (born 1920), Aberlour Orphanage, 1928–35.

38   D. Haynes, *Haste Ye Back* (London, Jarrolds, 1973), p. 76.

39   Correspondence with Dorothy (born 1949), Aberlour Orphanage, 1956–65.

40   SRO, ED 11/154: Committee on Homeless Children. Evidence of R. Cardno, 1946.

41   Interview with Arthur.

42   Interview with David.

43   SRO, ED 11/159: Committee on Homeless Children. The National Council of Women, Scottish Standing Committee, 1945.

44   Report of the Care of Children Committee (Curtis Report), *Parliamentary Papers*, 1945–46, (Cmd 6922).

45   SRO, ED 11/266: Committee on Homeless Children. Evidence of Mr Peter MacDonald, Governor of Dumbarton Townend Hospital, 1945.

46   Interview with Betty (born 1937), boarded out to Aberdeen, 1937–43, Tiree, 1943–56.

47 Ian Mac an Fhleisdeir (Tiree), interviewed on *Air Fasdadh*, BBC 2 Scotland, broadcast 1997.
48 Interview with Frances (born 1936), boarded out to Aberdeenshire, 1936–54.
49 Interview with Betty.
50 Interview with Robert (born 1934), boarded out to Banff, 1937–48.
51 Bernard Mac a'Ghobhainn (Tiree), interviewed on *Air Fasdadh*.
52 Interview with Betty.
53 GCA, D-CH 1/1: Children's Committee Minute Book, 1852–65.
54 'Report of the Departmental Committee appointed by the Local Government Board to Inquire into Existing Systems for the Maintenance and Education of Children (Mundella Report)', *Parliamentary Papers*, 1896 (C 8032), p. 590.
55 Correspondence with Frank (born 1938), boarded out in Aberdeenshire, 1939–53.
56 Correspondence with Eleanor (born 1933), boarded out in Aberdeenshire, 1934–48.
57 Pol MacCaluim (South Uist), interviewed on *Air Fasdadh*.
58 SRO, ED 11/168: Committee on Homeless Children. Report on Visit to Boarded-out Children around Inverness, 19 May 1946.
59 Interview with Peter (born 1934), boarded out on Black Isle, 1934–38, Invernessshire, 1938–49.
60 Eileen Leppard interviewed on *Air Fasdadh*
61 Interview with Peter.
62 *Ibid.*
63 Interview with Robert.
64 Interview with Annie.
65 Eileen Leppard, interviewed on *Air Fasdadh*.
66 Interview with Peter.

Index

Note: 'n.' after a page reference indicates a note number on that page.

see also sexual abuse
Cunningham, Hugh 2, 16, 78, 84, 91, 152

Davidoff, Leonore 126
Davin, Anna 134
Davis, Jennifer 138
Davis, Natalie Zemon 134
death
    children's attitudes towards 4, 8, 37–52 *passim*, 54n.12
    infant mortality rates 39–40
    of children 4, 37–8, 40–52 *passim*
Descartes, Rene 6–7
Dickens, Charles
    Bleak House 34n.19
Dod, John 67

education 8–9, 16–17, 19–22, 31, 40
    boarding schools 117–28 *passim*
    law 28
    Ragged schools 24, 36n.37
Esperance, Jeanne L' 126
Evelyn, John 46–7, 52

family life *see* parents
Fleetwood, William 61
Forman, Simon 62
Freud, Anna 160
Freud, Sigmund 156

games *see* play
Gouge, William 66–7

Hammerton, James 142–3, 147
Harris, Jose 119

Date Due

OC 22 '00			
SE 27 '0			
NO 8 '05			
AP 27 '06			
OCT 1 4 2009			